AF426506

HOPEFUL TRAVELER

TOPHER KEARBY

BE A HOPEFUL TRAVELER—
SOMEONE WHO UNDERSTANDS THAT
LIFE IS MORE ABOUT THE JOURNEY
THAN THE DESTINATION.

Hopeful Traveler

Copyright © 2024 by Topher Kearby

All rights reserved.

This is a work of fiction. Any resemblance to actual persons living or dead, businesses, events, or locales is purely coincidental. Reproduction in whole or part without the express written consent is strictly prohibited.

Cover Art by Topher Kearby

Art Copyright © 2024 by Topher Kearby

Cover Design Copyright © 2024 by Topher Kearby

Edited by Beth Cooper

www.TopherKearby.com

ISBN: 978-0-578-38146-6

Printed in the United States of America by Topher Kearby Inc.

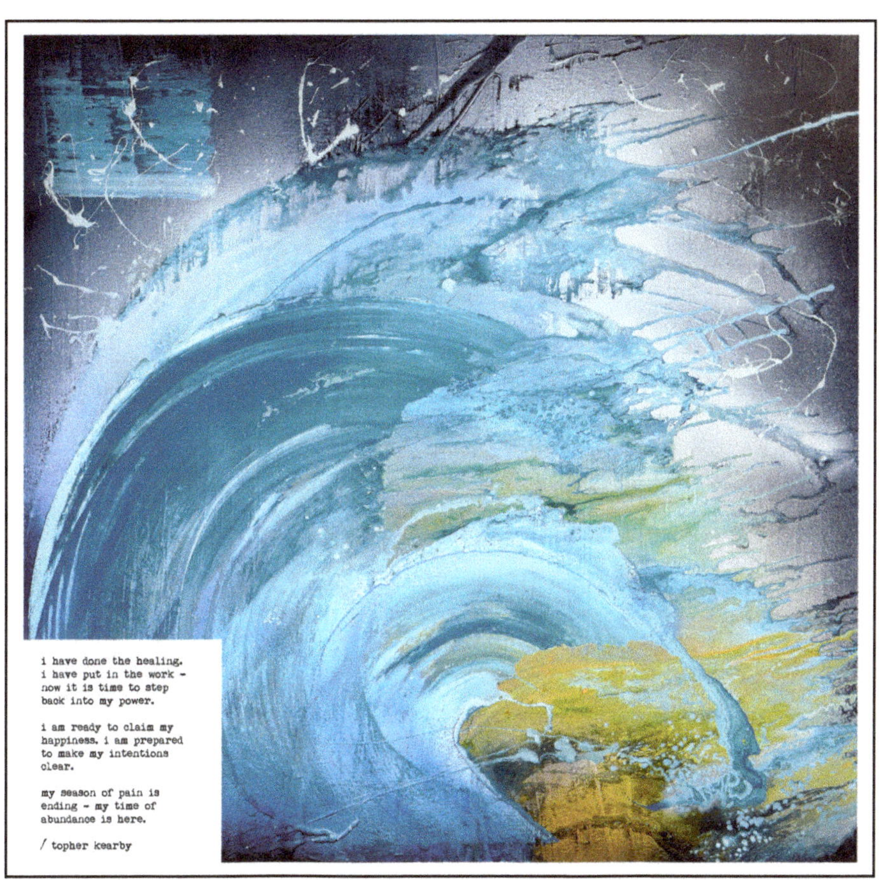

HOPEFUL TRAVELER

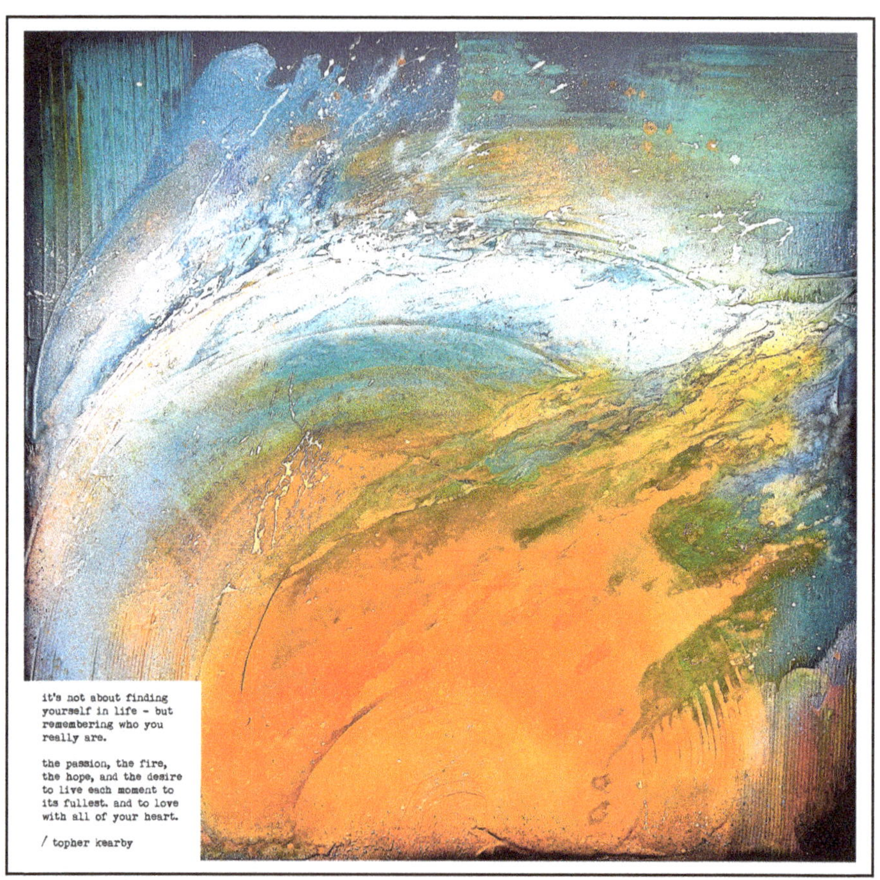
it's not about finding
yourself in life - but
remembering who you
really are.

the passion, the fire,
the hope, and the desire
to live each moment to
its fullest. and to love
with all of your heart.

/ topher kearby

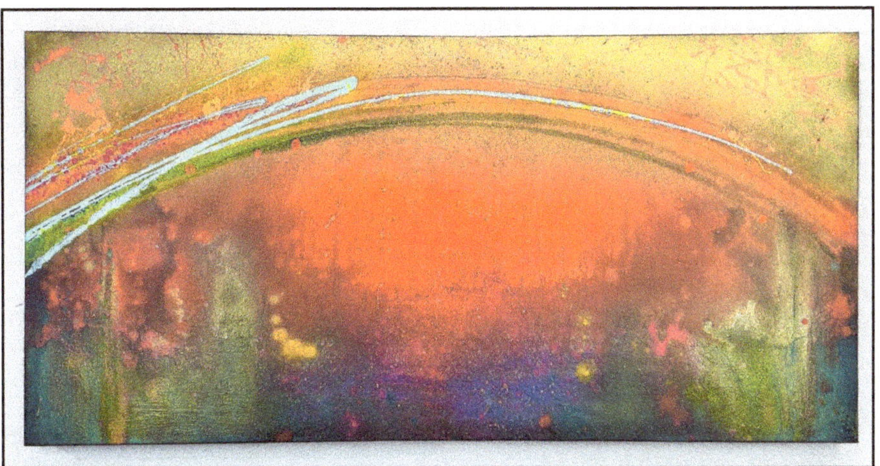

A few years ago I was working full time as a teacher – a job that I loved – and I was using all of my spare moments to go after my dream of becoming an artist and writer.

I also have two daughters that are my heart.

So, there was often so much going on that I barely noticed when day become night – I needed to make a change.

I made the difficult choice to step away from teaching and move toward a career built on my passions.

It was time.

I was ready.

But it wasn't a simple choice.

I didn't have it all planned out but I knew in my heart that if I gave this path everything I had it would end up exactly where I needed to be - it wouldn't be easy, but nothing good comes easily.

Taking away the responsibilities of teaching and planning did allow much more time to paint, write, and create. But I actually ended up spending even less time away from work. I was loving my journey but it was all-consuming.

Perhaps it's my personality or more likely it is just what it takes to get a small business off the ground, but I was working almost every moment I was awake.

I loved what I was doing so much that it was all I could think about.

I was making progress with my career but I was missing out on life.

Finally, one evening I was sitting in my backyard watching the sunset as my girls played and it hit me.

I remember thinking, "I need more of this."

So, I made a plan that no matter what I was doing I would be done in time to watch the sunset in the backyard.

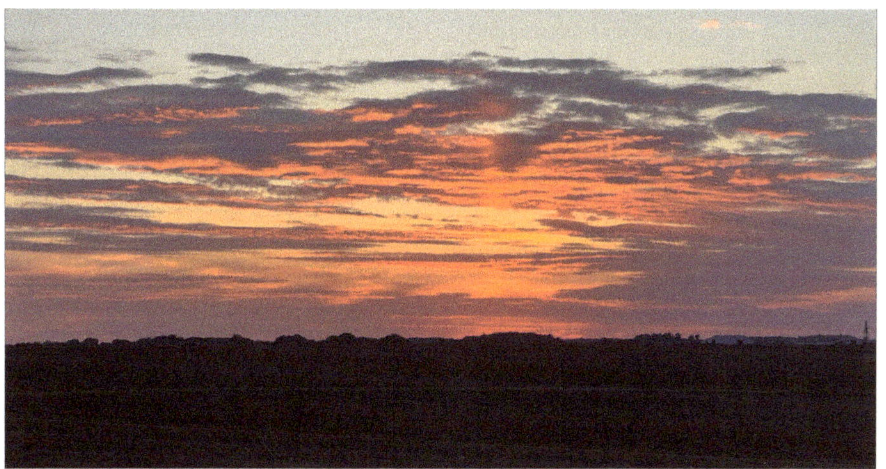

The days were longer at the time so it was a small goal but it made a huge impact in my life.

Of course I wasn't perfect with hitting my target at first but I did my best and over time it became the most important part of my day. Even when it was just me and my chair at the end of the day I would still take the time to watch the colors crawl across the sky.

It became so much more than time away from work. It became a time to reflect, recharge, and express gratitude for everything that had happened during the day.

I get delayed with my progress at times because I tend to think that every change needs to be something huge and dynamic. I need to burn it all down and start again or else I feel like I am not really doing anything with my full heart. This story is a perfect example of how that way of thinking can be destructive. A single decision ended up recharging my spirit in such a meaningful way that I am still feeling the effects to this day.

Yes, sometimes life requires big choices in order to get where we need to go. But more often it requires far less.

I still do my best to watch the sunset each night no matter where I am. Even if it is just for a moment. It will forever be my reminder to take life a little more slowly and to appreciate the time I have on this earth more fully.

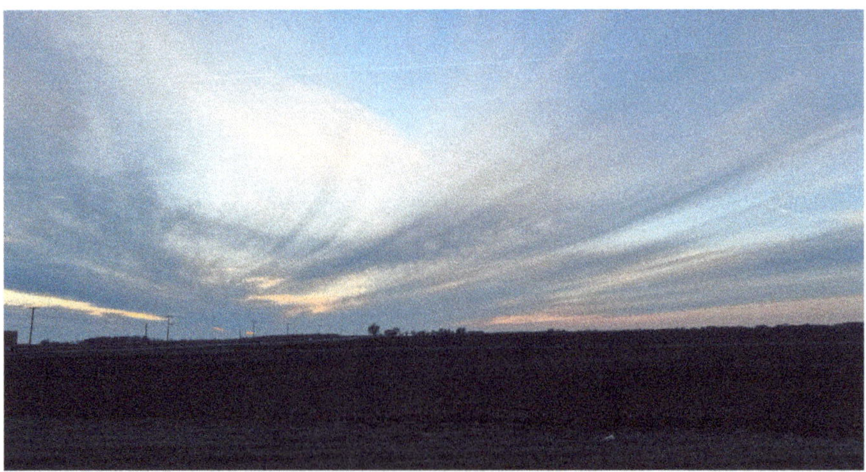

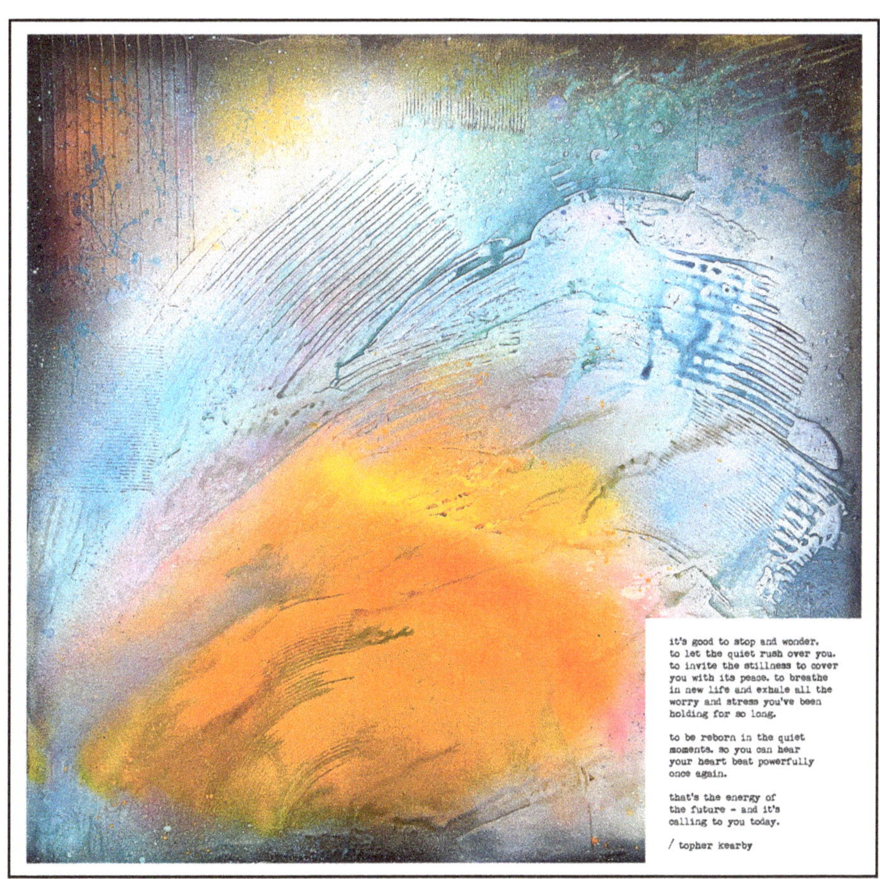

HOPEFUL TRAVELER

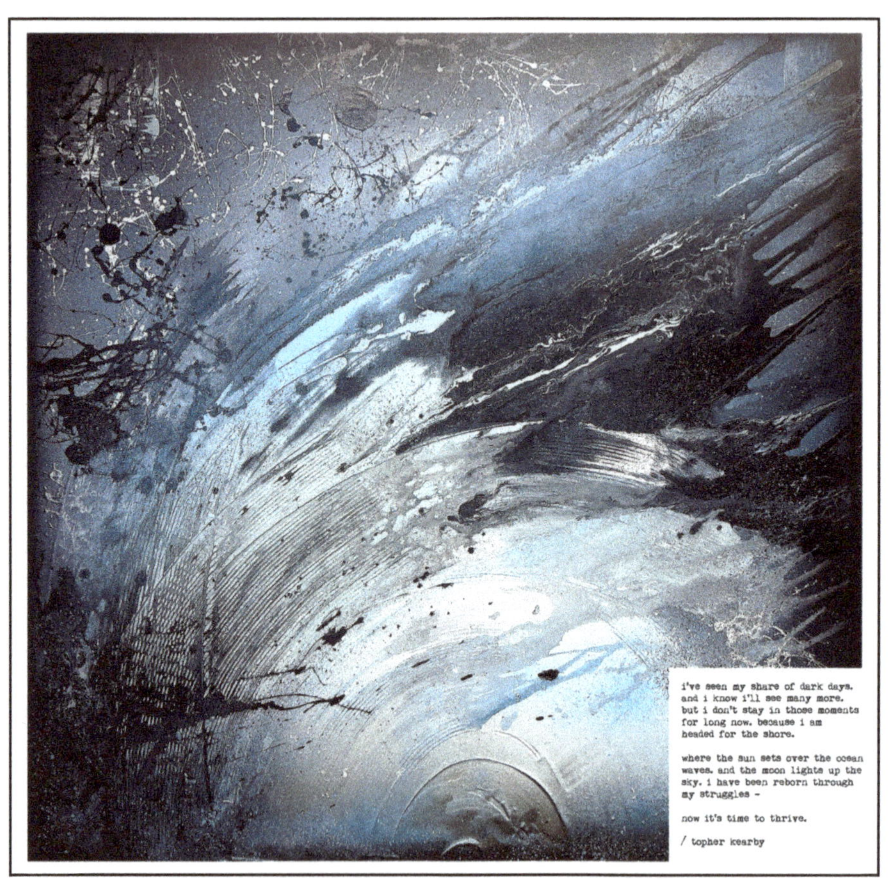

i've seen my share of dark days.
and i know i'll see many more.
but i don't stay in those moments
for long now. because i am
headed for the shore.

where the sun sets over the ocean
waves. and the moon lights up the
sky. i have been reborn through
my struggles -

now it's time to thrive.

/ topher kearby

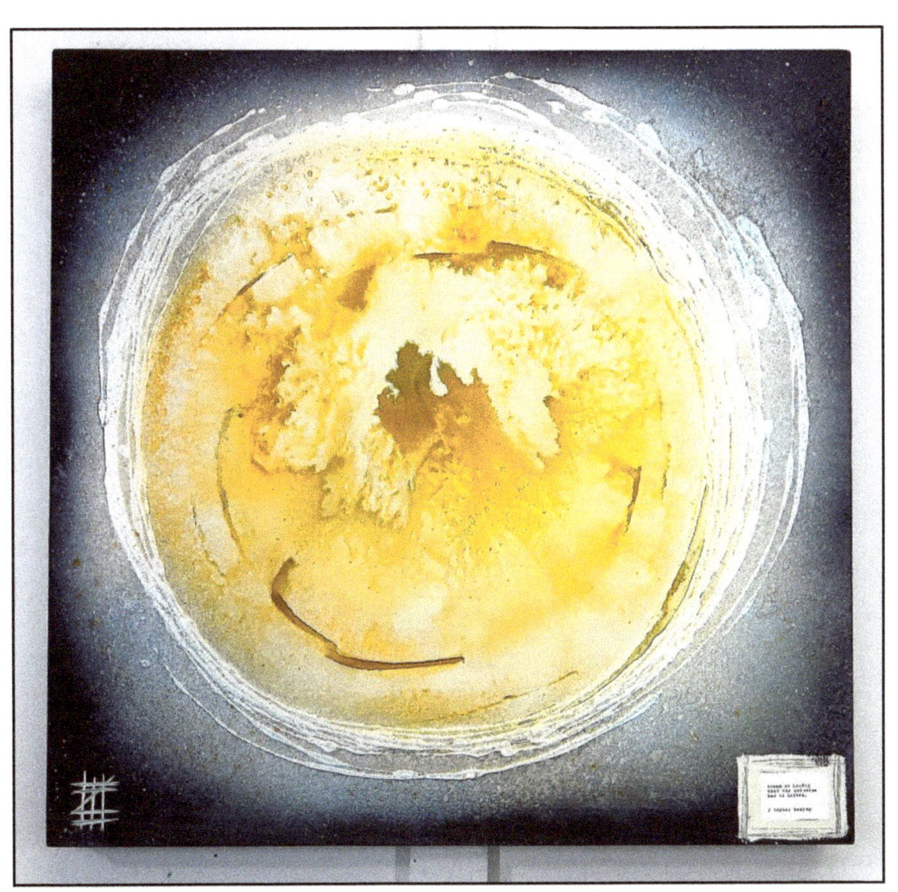

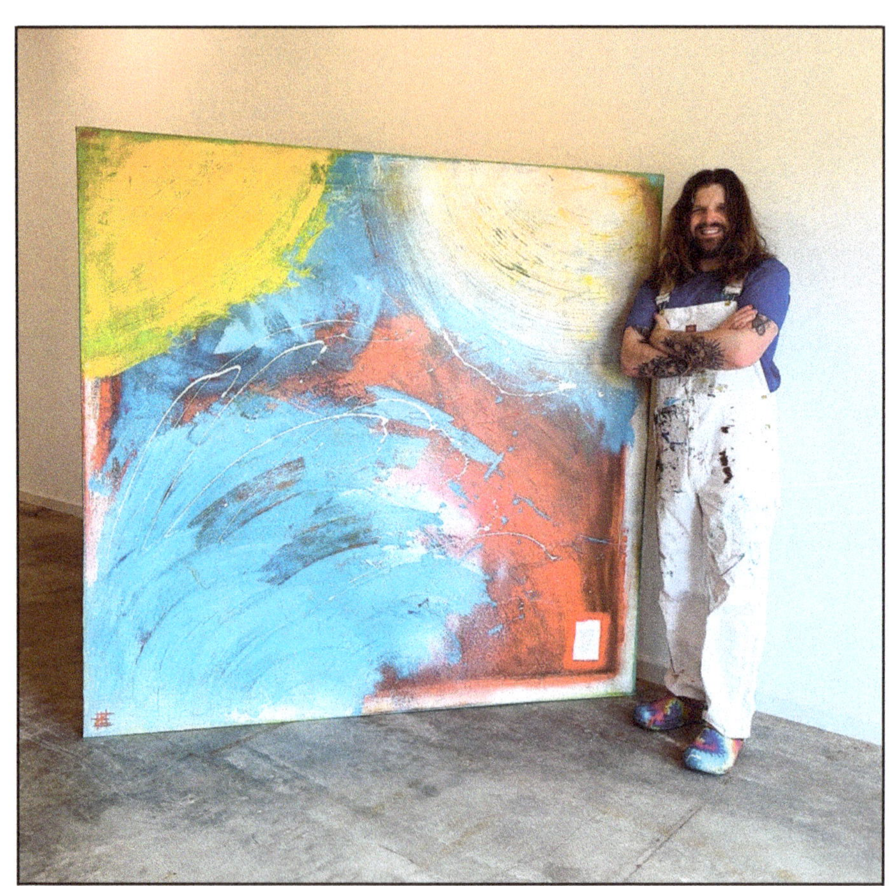

i used to be trapped in my own
worry. about the future. about
the worst-case scenario. i
would tell myself that i was
protecting my future -
but i wasn't.

i was creating a prison in my
"now" in hopes that it would
bring me freedom some time up
ahead. it never really works
out like that. because the
present is all we have. these
moments we are living - now.

and if we constantly sacrifice
them for a "better" tomorrow
then we will never experience
the full beauty of today.

/ topher kearby

we are born dreamers.

our hearts long to beat
with the passion that is
only found when we are
brave enough to get lost
for a while.

so, let's take hold of
that energy and go find
our adventure and our
purpose. because through
that journey we discover
the true wonder of life.

/ topher kearby

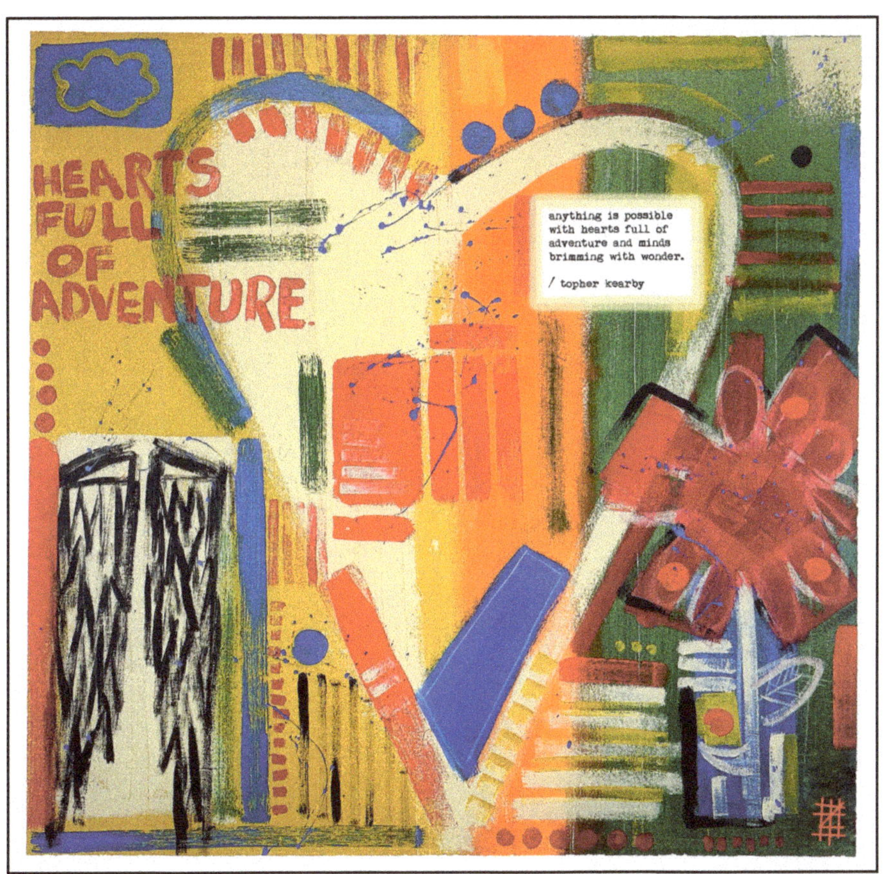

HEARTS
FULL
OF
ADVENTURE.

anything is possible
with hearts full of
adventure and minds
brimming with wonder.

/ topher kearby

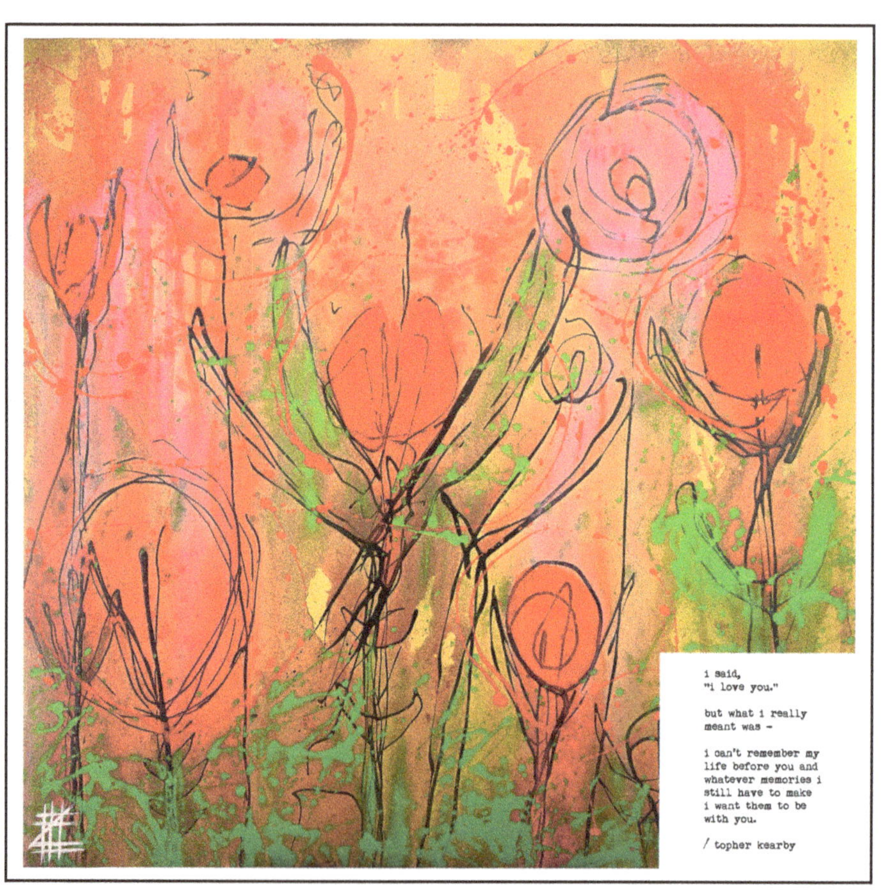
i said,
"i love you."

but what i really
meant was –

i can't remember my
life before you and
whatever memories i
still have to make
i want them to be
with you.

/ topher kearby

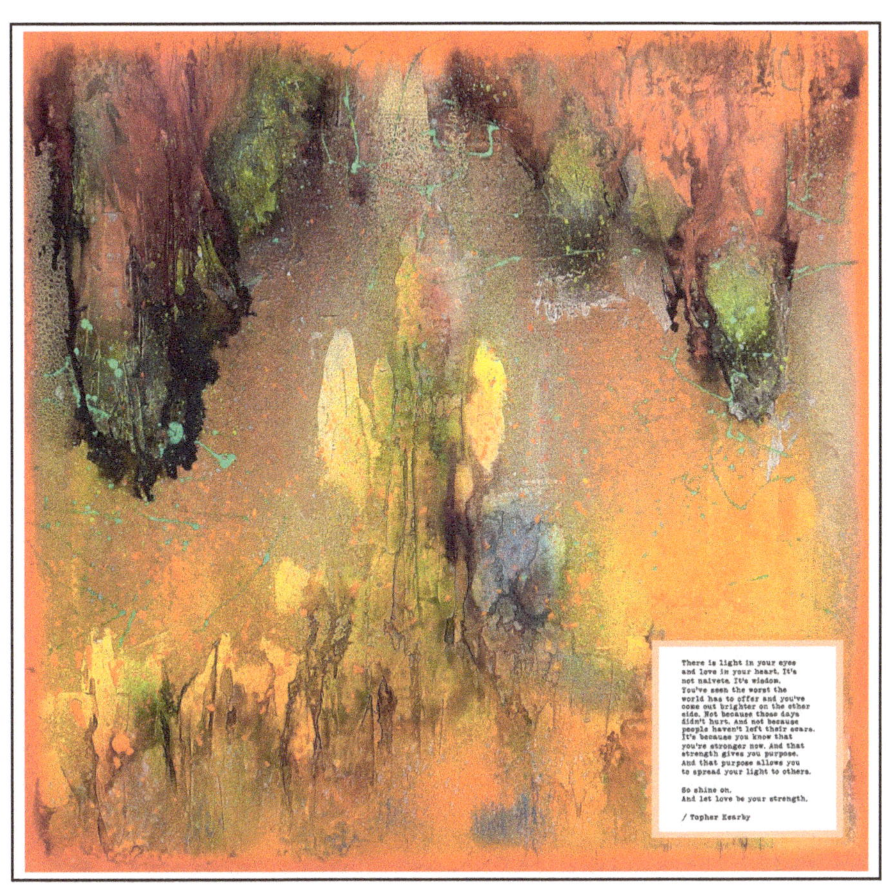

There is light in your eyes
and love in your heart. It's
not naivete. It's wisdom.
You've seen the worst the
world has to offer and you've
come out brighter on the other
side. Not because those days
didn't hurt. And not because
people haven't left their scars.
It's because you know that
you're stronger now. And that
strength gives you purpose.
And that purpose allows you
to spread your light to others.

So shine on.
And let love be your strength.

/ Topher Kearby

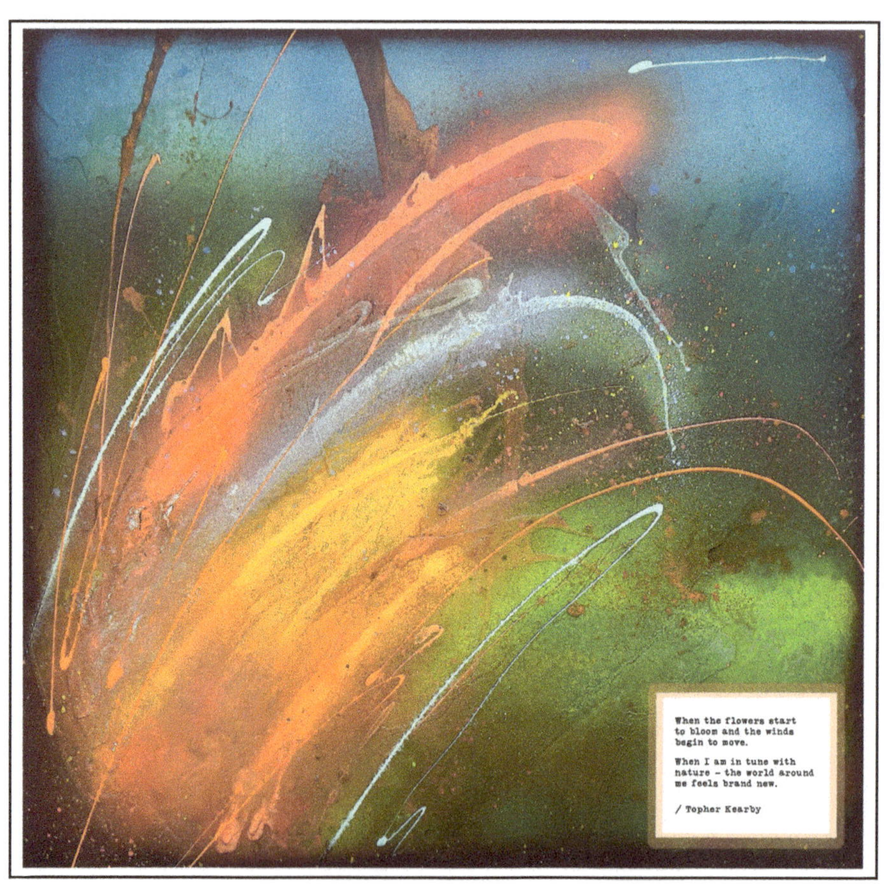

When the flowers start
to bloom and the winds
begin to move.

When I am in tune with
nature – the world around
me feels brand new.

/ Topher Kearby

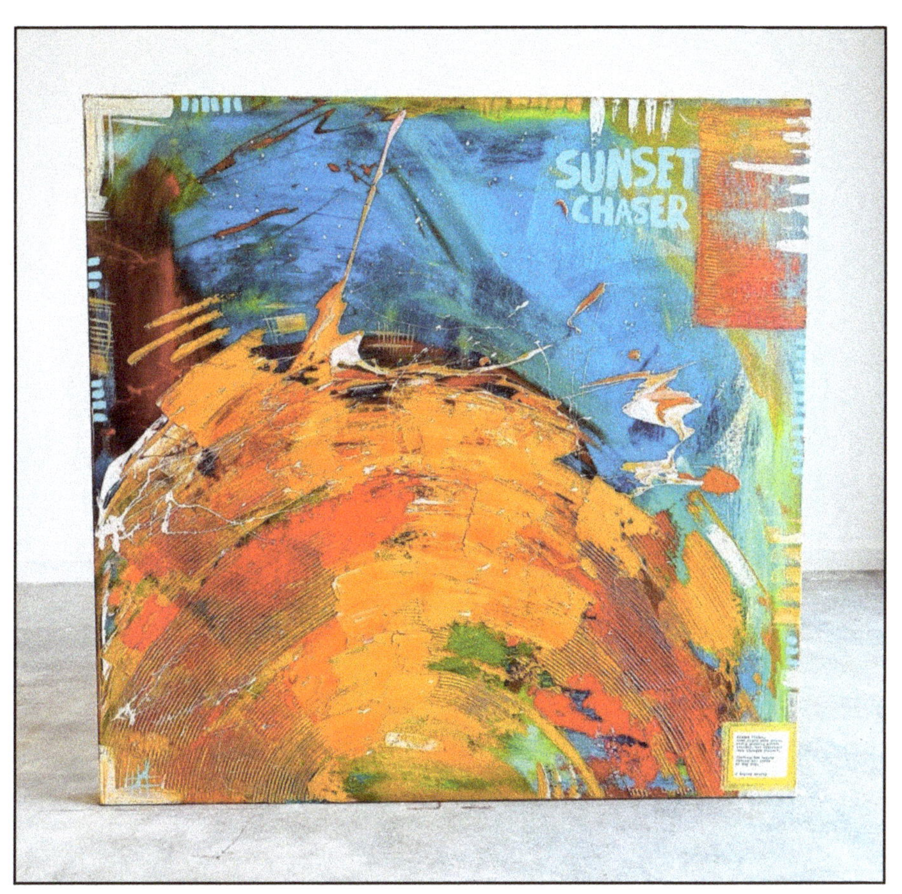

SUNSET
CHASER

sunset chaser,
late night star gazer,
early morning coffee
drinker, and afternoon
deep thought thinker.

finding the beauty
during all parts
of the day.

/ topher kearby

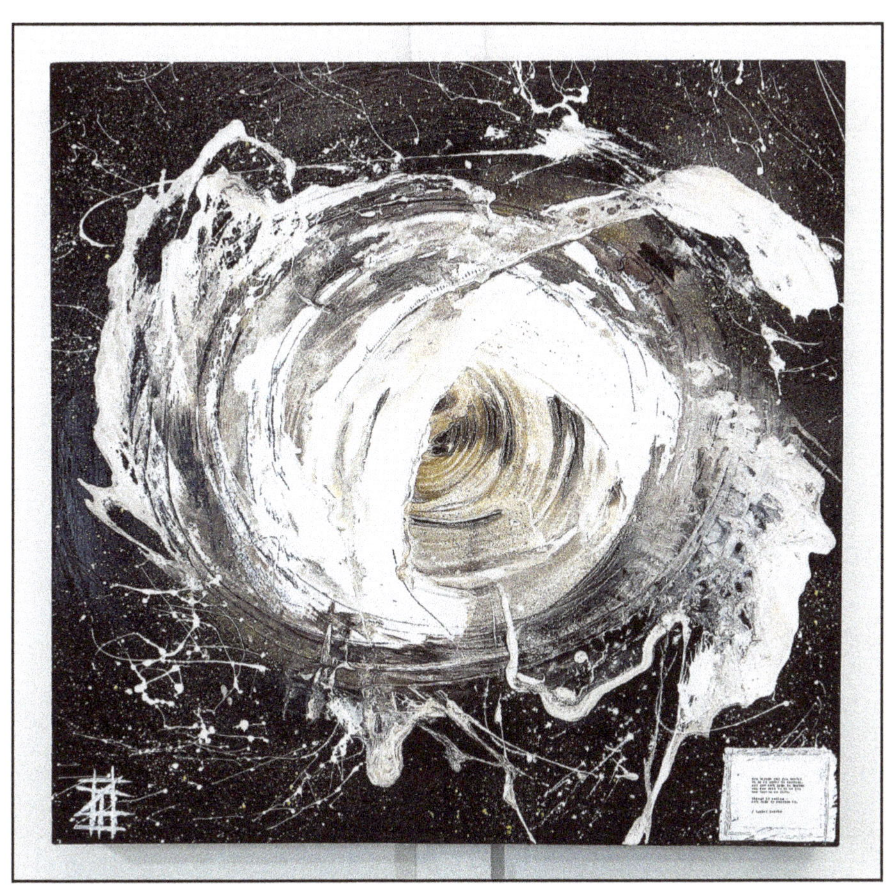

We feel better when we have a purpose, and for many that is found through our interactions with others.

Maybe it's family, friends, or a community. We desire to add to the story of life by offering what we have and who we are.

And that's beautiful.

However, that pursuit can grow negative when we feel we must bring something other than what we have to be accepted –

"What I have is not enough."

"Who I am is not enough."

"I have nothing special to offer."

Thoughts like the ones above can be so heavy to carry. I have thought them more time than I care to remember. But true power comes when we realize we are who we are for a reason. We have the skills we have for a reason. And when we tap into that energy we are able to give others the greatest gift of all – hope.

And that hope travels far beyond this lifetime and keeps making an impact long after we are gone.

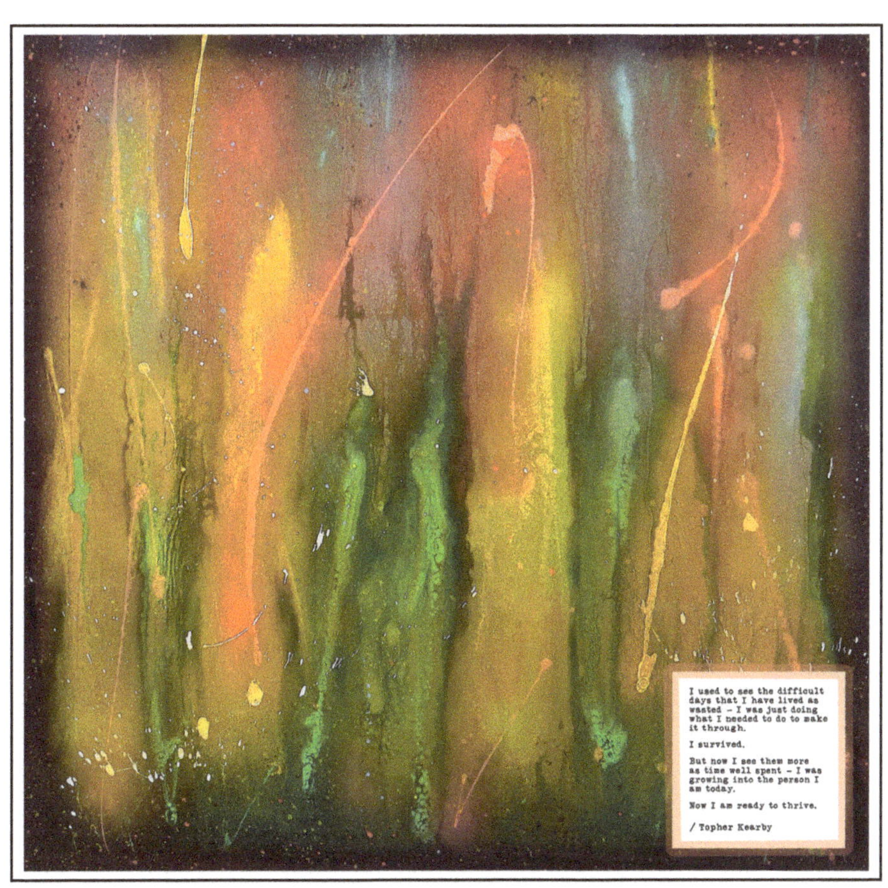

I used to see the difficult
days that I have lived as
wasted — I was just doing
what I needed to do to make
it through.

I survived.

But now I see them more
as time well spent — I was
growing into the person I
am today.

Now I am ready to thrive.

/ Topher Kearby

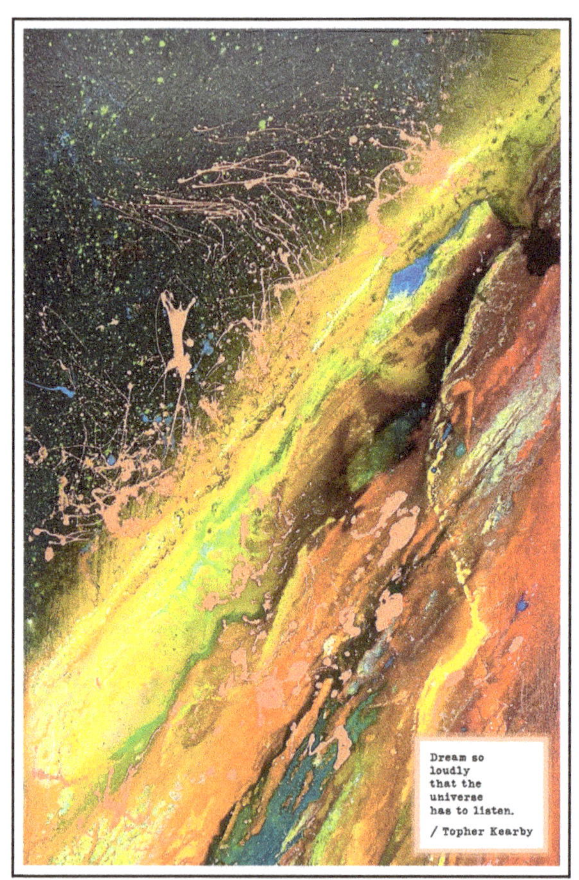
Dream so
loudly
that the
universe
has to listen.

/ Topher Kearby

when we love people as they are,
where they are, for who they are
- life becomes simple. no longer
are assumptions clouding our
vision. because we see that
people are doing the best with
what they have been given.

forgiveness replaces
resentment. and kindness
overcomes any judgments.

it's a better way to live
and it keeps life simple -
love first, love more, and
appreciate people for who
they really are.

/ topher kearby

protect your happiness by
surrounding yourself with
people who love you, and
with passions that keep
you moving forward
on your journey.

the influences we allow
into our lives matter —
so, let's make sure they
are ones that elevate our
dreams and keep us honest
to our true selves.

/ topher kearby

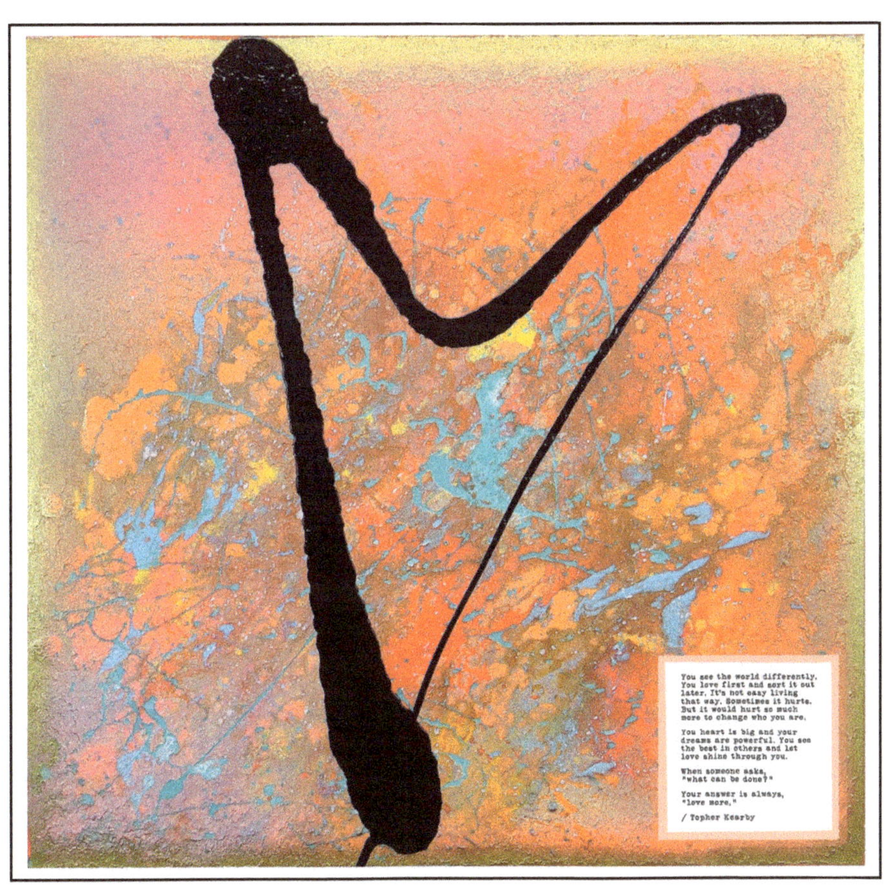

You see the world differently.
You love first and sort it out
later. It's not easy living
that way. Sometimes it hurts.
But it would hurt so much
more to change who you are.

You heart is big and your
dreams are powerful. You see
the best in others and let
love shine through you.

When someone asks,
"what can be done?"

Your answer is always,
"love more,"

/ Topher Kearby

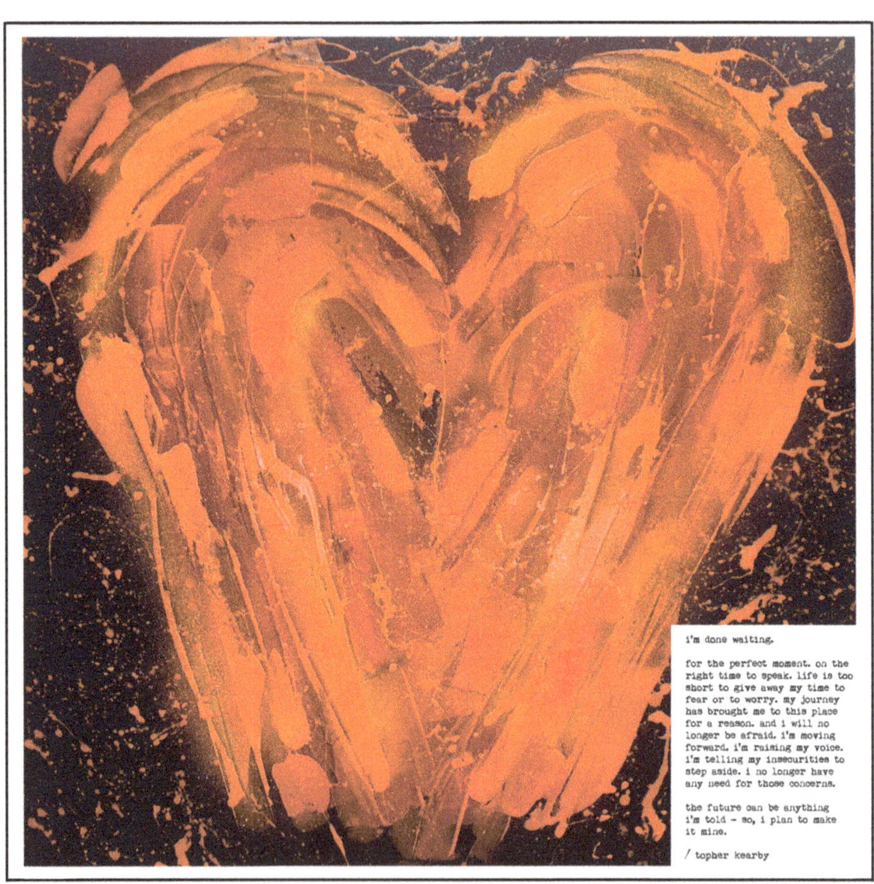

i'm done waiting.

for the perfect moment. on the
right time to speak. life is too
short to give away my time to
fear or to worry. my journey
has brought me to this place
for a reason. and i will no
longer be afraid. i'm moving
forward. i'm raising my voice.
i'm telling my insecurities to
step aside. i no longer have
any need for those concerns.

the future can be anything
i'm told - so, i plan to make
it mine.

/ topher kearby

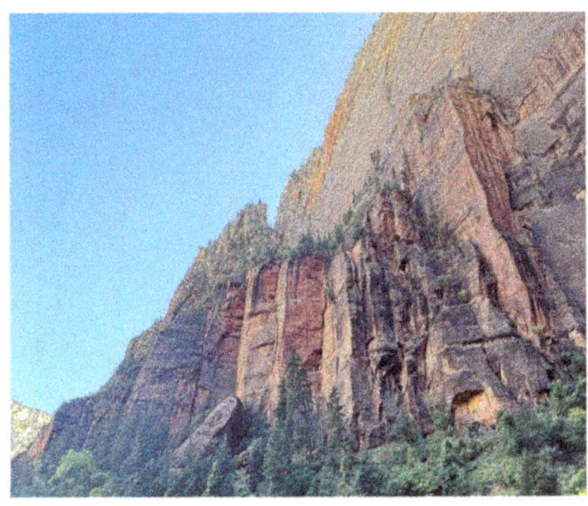

Memories matter –

The moments where our minds are blown away with the beauty of a mountain sunset.

Or the times when our souls are put at ease by the crashing of the ocean's waves.

Memories lift us when life gets hard, and we make them when we get out of our normal routines and experience something new.

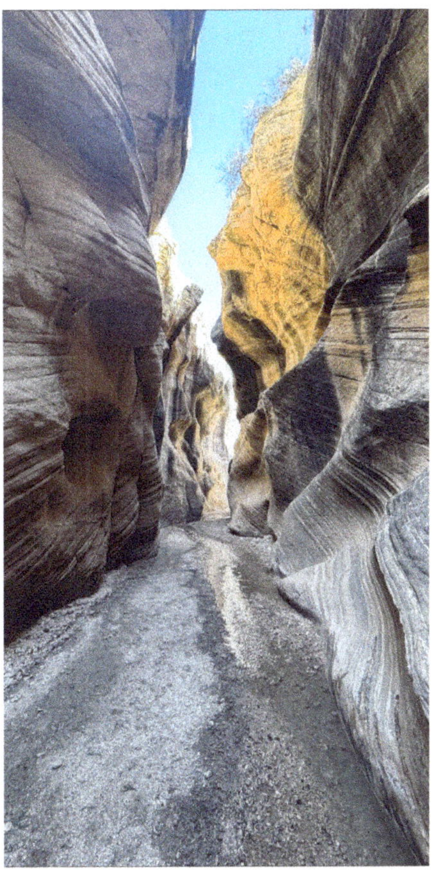

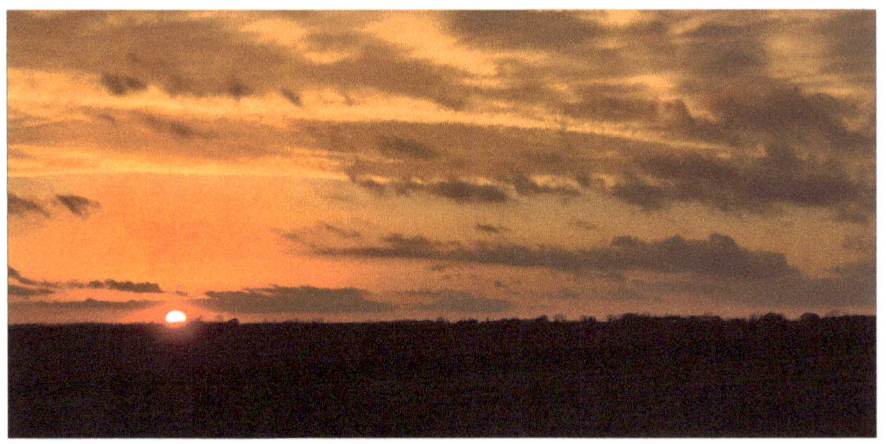

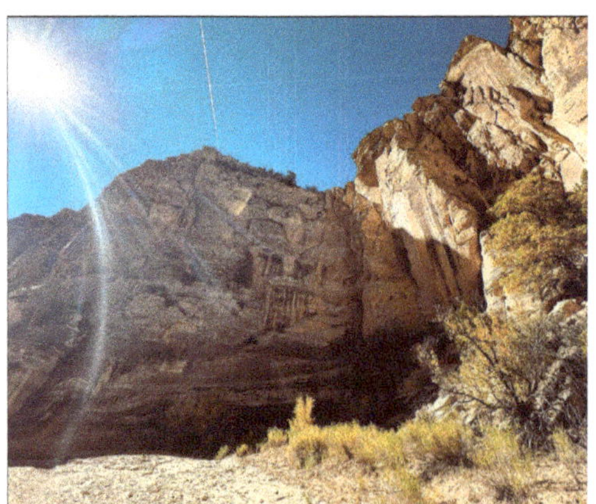

we need others to need us;
that doesn't make us weak.

it makes us human.

/ topher kearby

we are born with a fire
within us – it's the magic
that brings purpose to
our lives.

the more we understand
it and tap into its power
the more fulfilling our
lives become.

so let's burn brightly
and allow our passions
to light the way to
true happiness.

/ topher kearby

there are those who
promise to be there
for you, but then
they never are.

and there are those
who don't need to say
a thing, because they
are already standing
beside you.

/ topher kearby

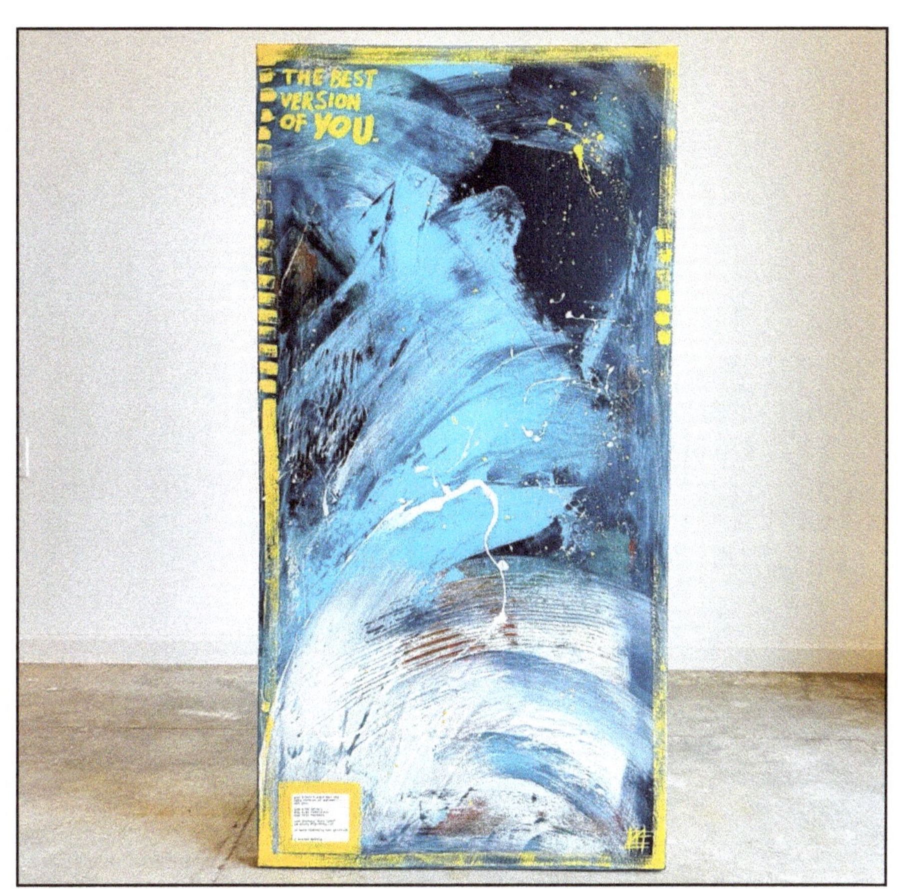

THE BEST
VERSION
OF YOU.

you haven't even met the
best version of yourself -
not yet.

the most healed.
the most fulfilled.
the most content.

and meeting that "you"
is worth fighting for.

so keep learning and growing.

/ topher kearby

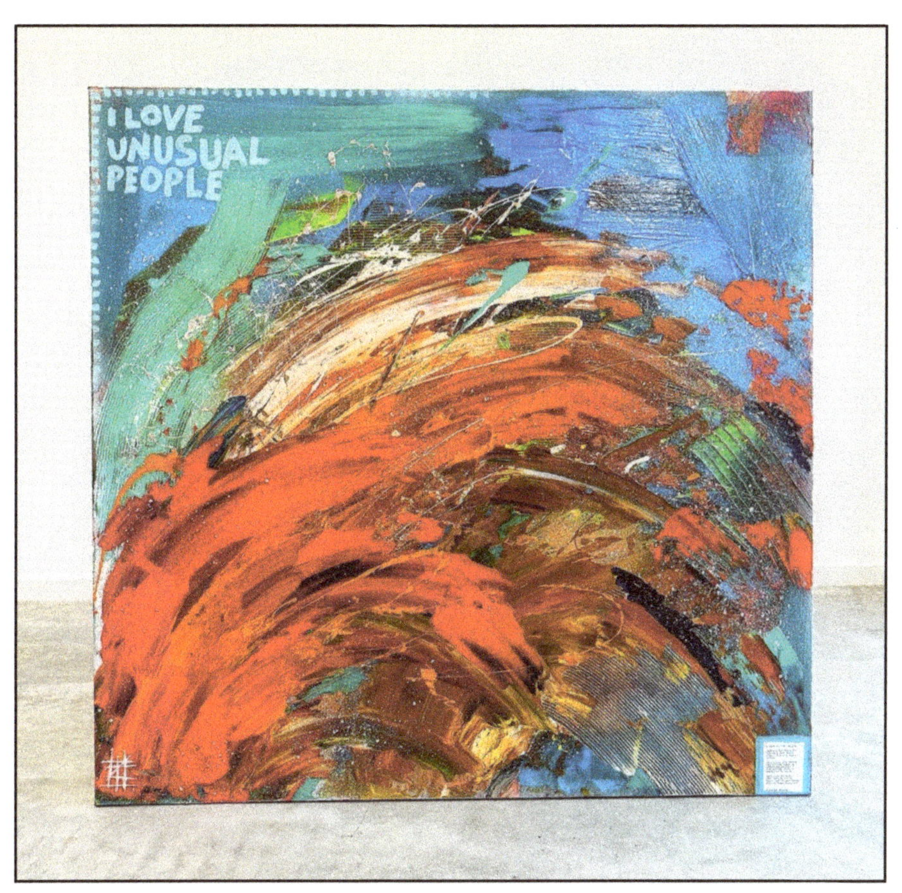
I LOVE
UNUSUAL
PEOPLE

i love unusual people.

ones who see the world
not only with their vision
but with their hearts.

people who love others
not because there is
something to gain –
but because there is
something to share.

they love quickly,
feel deeply, and do
their best to see others
for who they truly are.

/ topher kearby

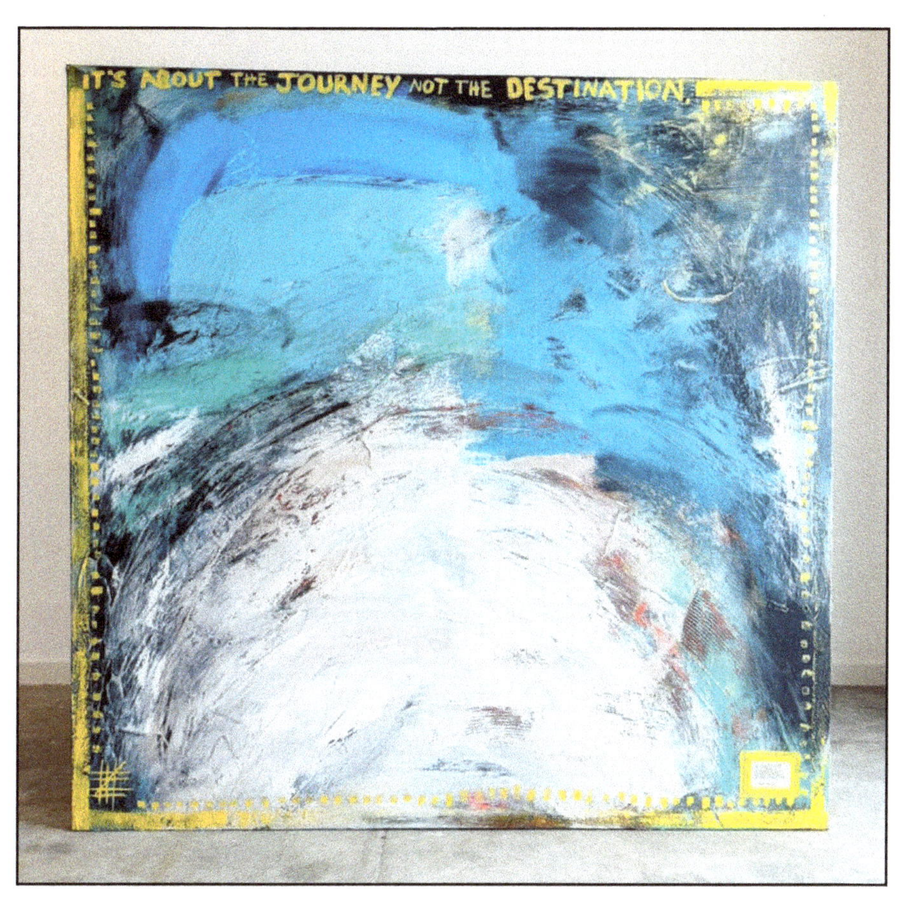

HOPEFUL TRAVELER

it's often the places
we didn't plan to go
and the people we
didn't know we needed
to meet that end up
changing our lives in
the most beautiful ways.

/ topher kearby

love people as they are,
but also love them as
they change and grow.

/ topher kearby

we don't need big events
or grand gestures to feel
connected –

doing nothing feels like
everything when you are
sharing those moments
with the people you love.

/ topher kearby

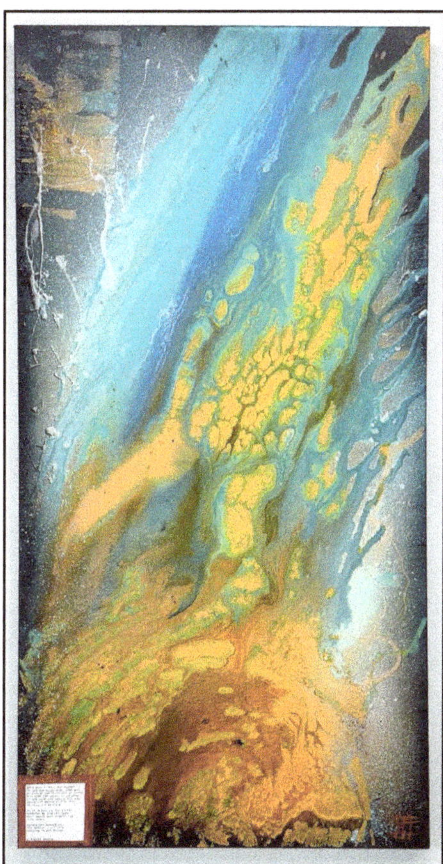

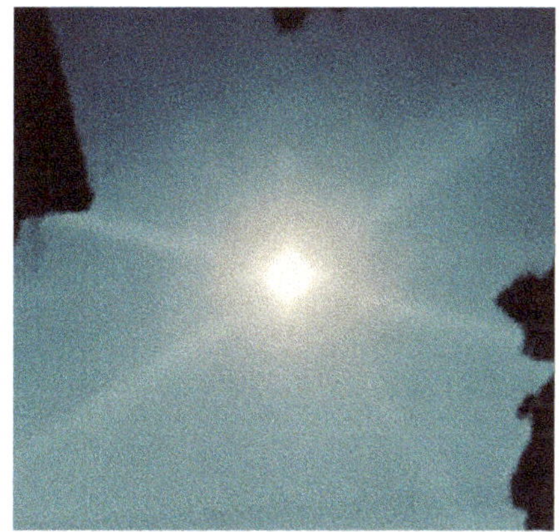

loving you has brought
back the pieces of me
that i didn't realize
were missing.

with you —
i finally feel whole.

/ topher kearby

SOME OF US ARE WEEDS –
WE KNOW HOW TO GROW IN THE DIFFICULT PLACES.

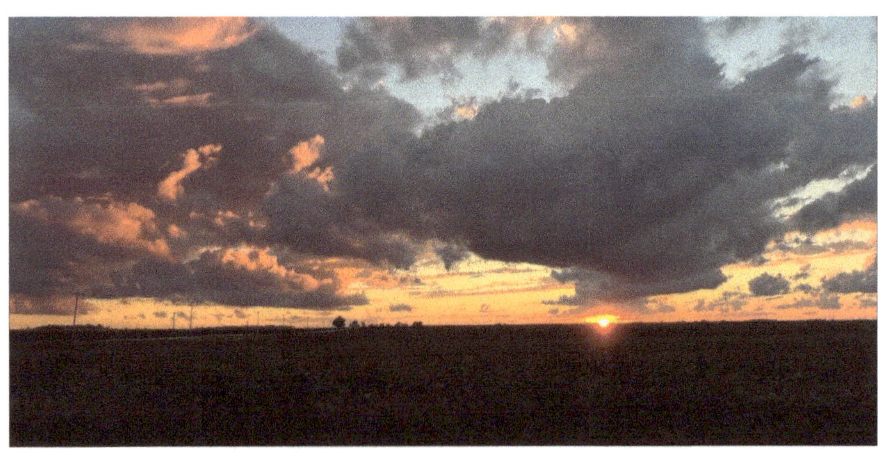

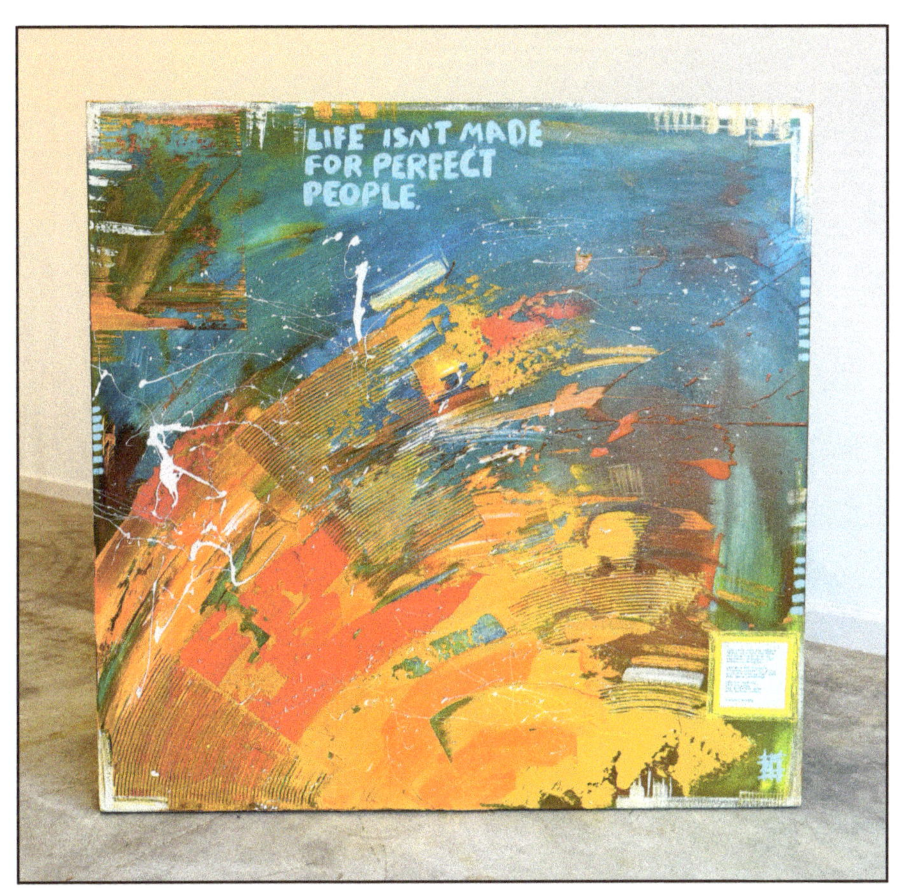

LIFE ISN'T MADE
FOR PERFECT
PEOPLE.

life isn't made for perfect
people. it's made for those
who know how to turn an
impossible situation into
something beautiful.

it's made for fighters.
dreamers. lovers. and people
who won't give up even when
life feels impossible.

it's not perfect.
it's not easy.
but that's why we're
made so damn tough.

/ topher kearby

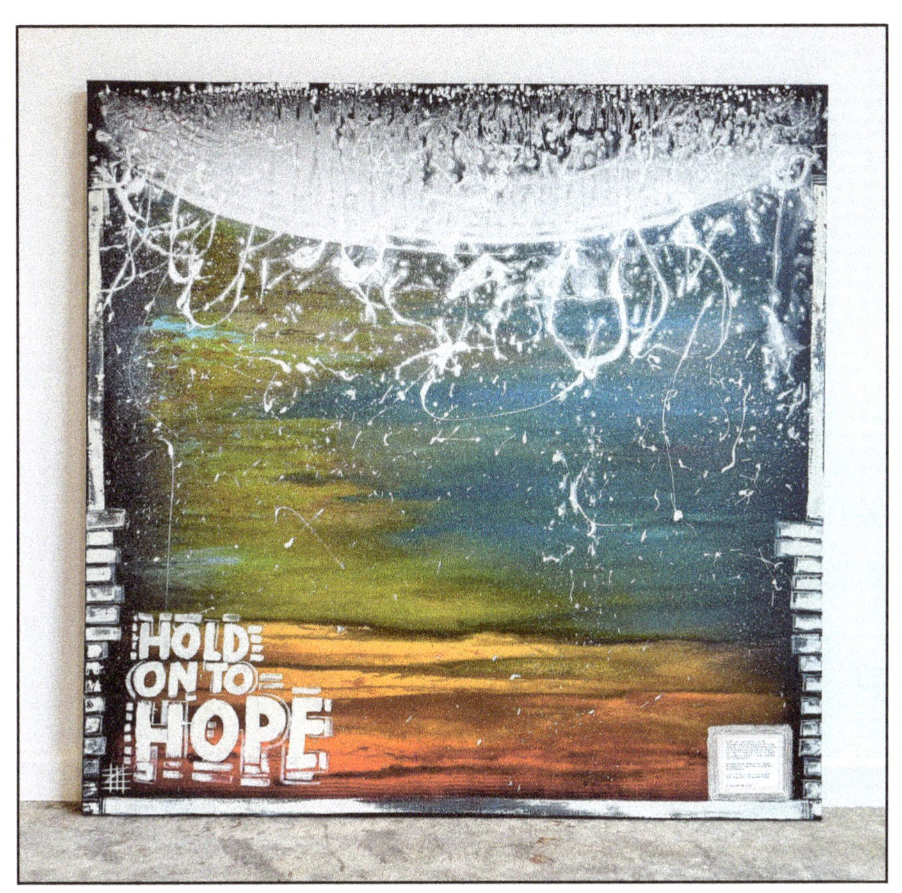

HOLD
ON TO
HOPE

hope is a powerful gift.
because it allows you to look
beyond what is currently going
on – maybe struggle or pain,
and see a future that is full
of possibilities – joy, wonder,
and adventure.

that's what makes our days
so special and our lives so
meaningful.

hold on to hope – it paves
the way for brighter days.

/ topher kearby

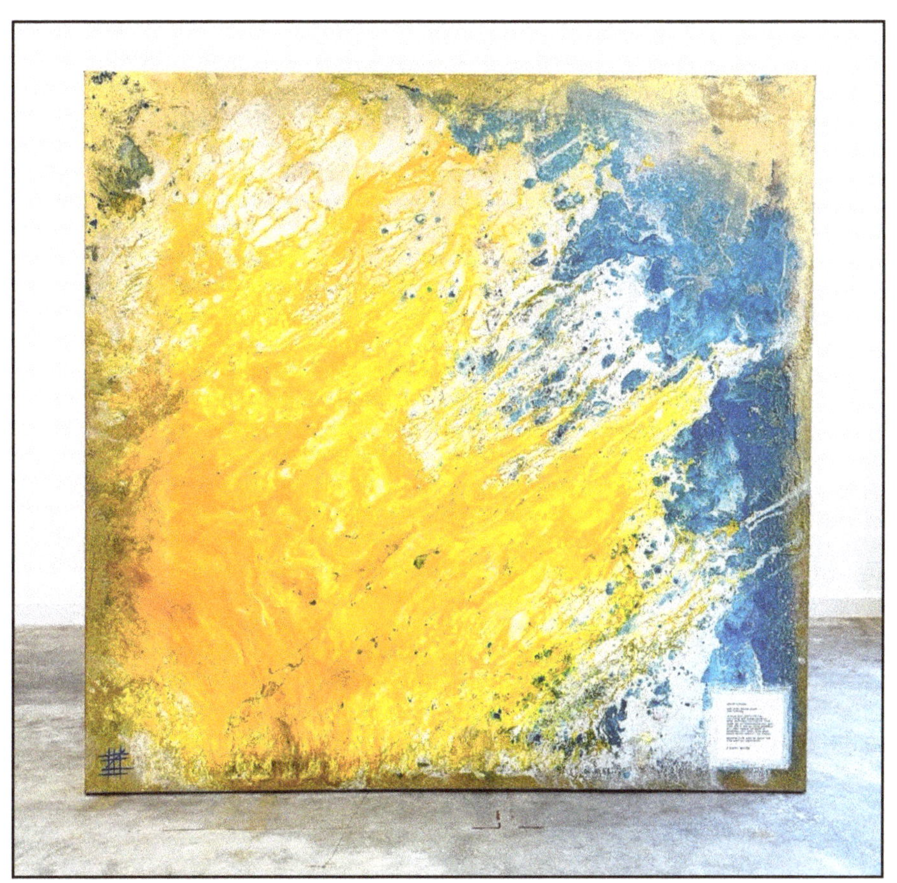

HOPEFUL TRAVELER

start living.

not just being alive -
but living.

wildly and wonderfully.
lovingly and passionately.
make mistakes and learn from
them. go on adventures and get
lost for a while. find yourself
all over again as much as
possible. and love with your
whole heart even if it hurts.

because life may be short but
it's also so important.

/ topher kearby

it's not about being happy
all the time. or being sure
of all your choices. it's
about knowing that life
is precious. even when it's
tough. that our days are
meaningful. even when
they feel like a fight.

like bob ross said,
"we don't make mistakes,
just happy little accidents."

it's learning to take what
could have destroyed you
and turn it into something
that helps you grow.

/ topher kearby

the greatest gift you
can give the people in
your life is to encourage
them to do great things.

be their cheerleader.
a voice of positivity that
encourages them to go after
their dreams. hold them up
when they feel like falling
over. to be a positive voice
in a world of often negative
noise and distraction.

it's important to stand
tall for the people you
love. to have their back.
and see them for who they
really are — someone who
can do amazing things.

/ topher kearby

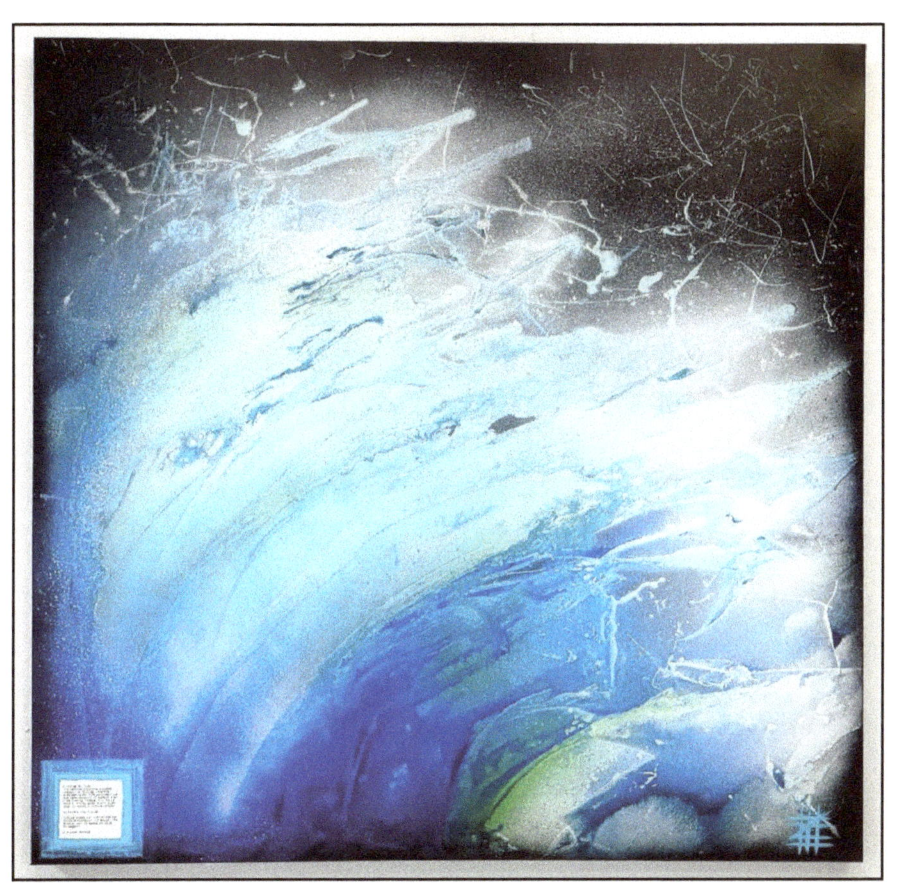

HOPEFUL TRAVELER

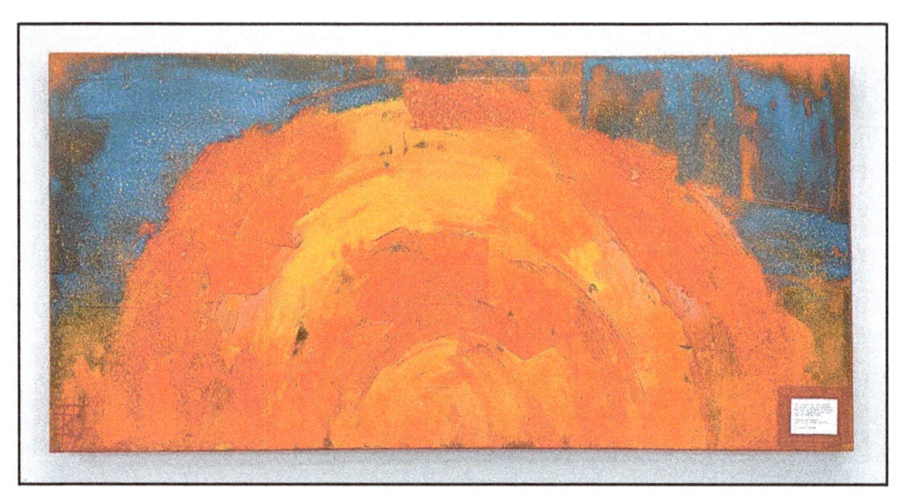

I'VE PUT IN THE WORK.
I'VE PUT IN THE TIME.
MY SEASON OF PAIN IS ENDING.
NOW IS MY TIME TO THRIVE.

we all know how hard it is to try and
keep it together when we're actually
falling apart. because life doesn't always
give us a pause. or a break in the action
in order for us to fix ourselves enough to
move forward completely. so we stumble
around a bit. we hurt longer than we
should. and we end up healing slowly.

but the thing is, that's okay. you and me
and everyone else experience those moments
the same. so that's why it's a good idea to
extend a bit of grace to others. because
we don't know what they're going through.
what they're overcoming. or the battles
they've been given to fight.

so let's share love. give kindness.
and help each other in the ways we can.

/ topher kearby

so often the best experiences
in life are detours. events
that take place just off the
standard path. moments that
we never planned or expected.
but they change us forever.
and help us see the world in
a new light.

/ topher kearby

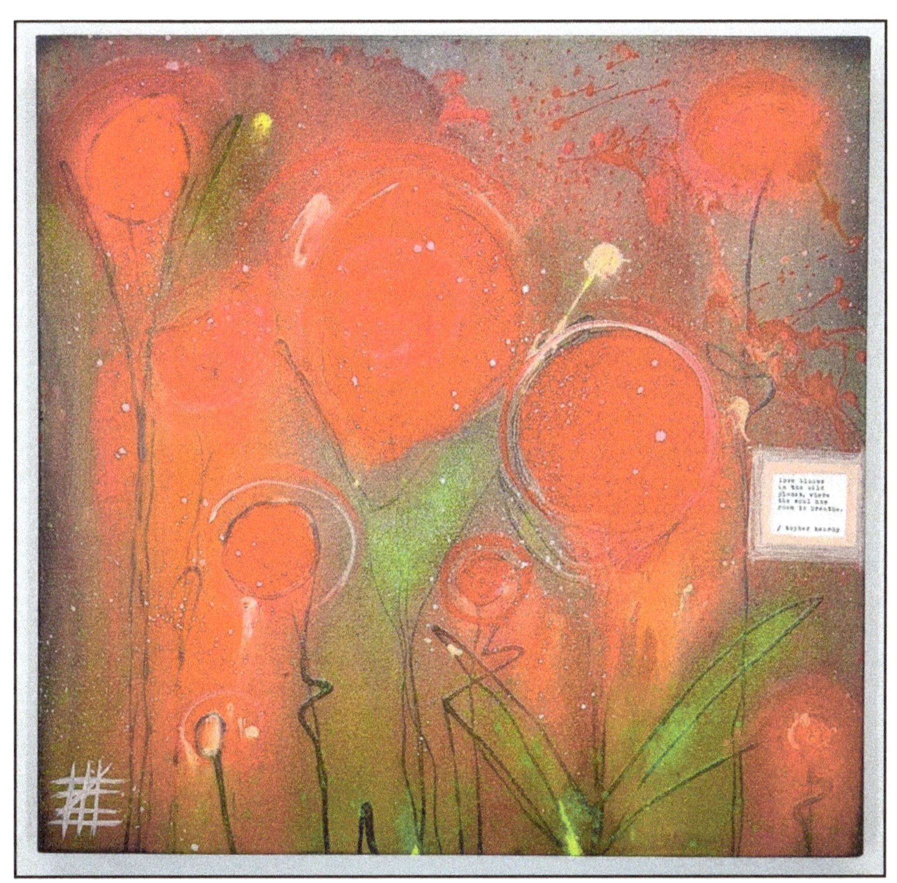

love blooms
in the wild
places, where
the soul has
room to breathe.

/ Sopher Hendry

love blooms
in the wild
places, where
the soul has
room to breathe.

/ topher kearby

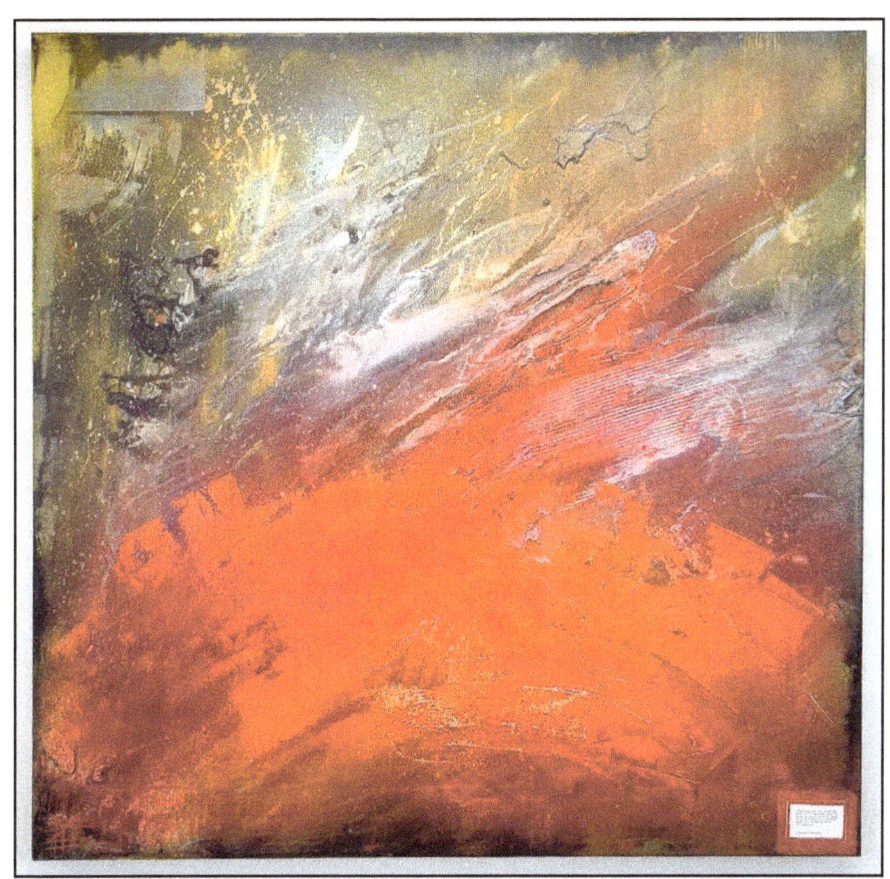

HOPEFUL **TRAVELER**

it's amazing the distance
you can cross when you've
made up your mind to keep
moving forward no matter
what you have to do to
make it through.

/ topher kearby

love is providing
a safe place for
loss and pain to
heal. and for hope
and joy to grow.

/ topher kearby

i said, "i love you."

but what i meant was —

i'm thankful i get a glimpse
of the world through your eyes.

how you see everything as
possible and everyone as
someone with an important
story to tell.

/ topher kearby

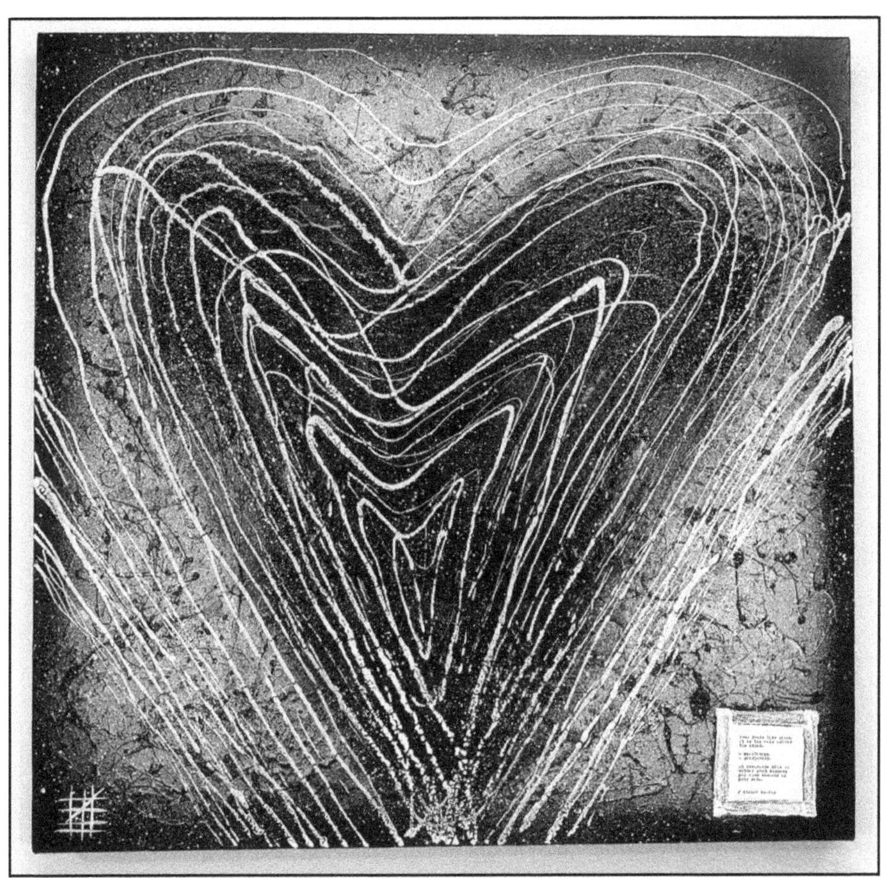

i said, "i love you."

but what i meant was —

i've never felt so much peace
with another person. i can rest
my mind and speak my heart for
the first time without feeling
judged or unwanted. i feel safe
with you. i feel known. and for
the first time i understand
what real love is.

/ topher kearby

i am not lost —

i am here to explore
the wild places where
most will never go.

/ topher kearby

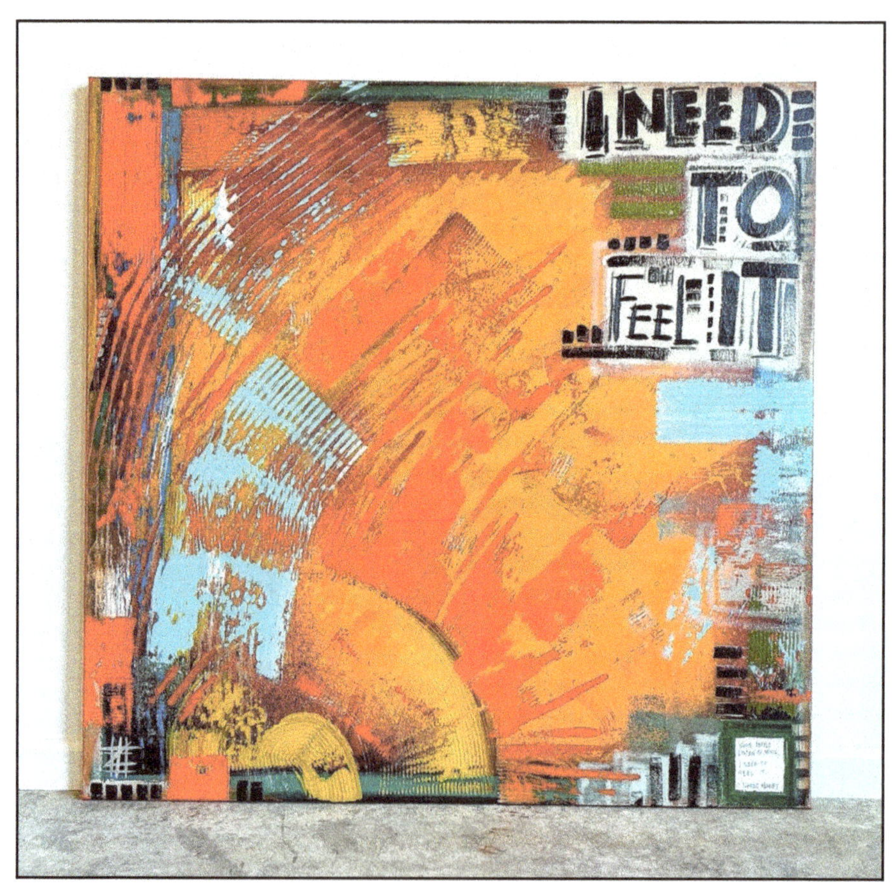

I NEED
TO
FEEL IT

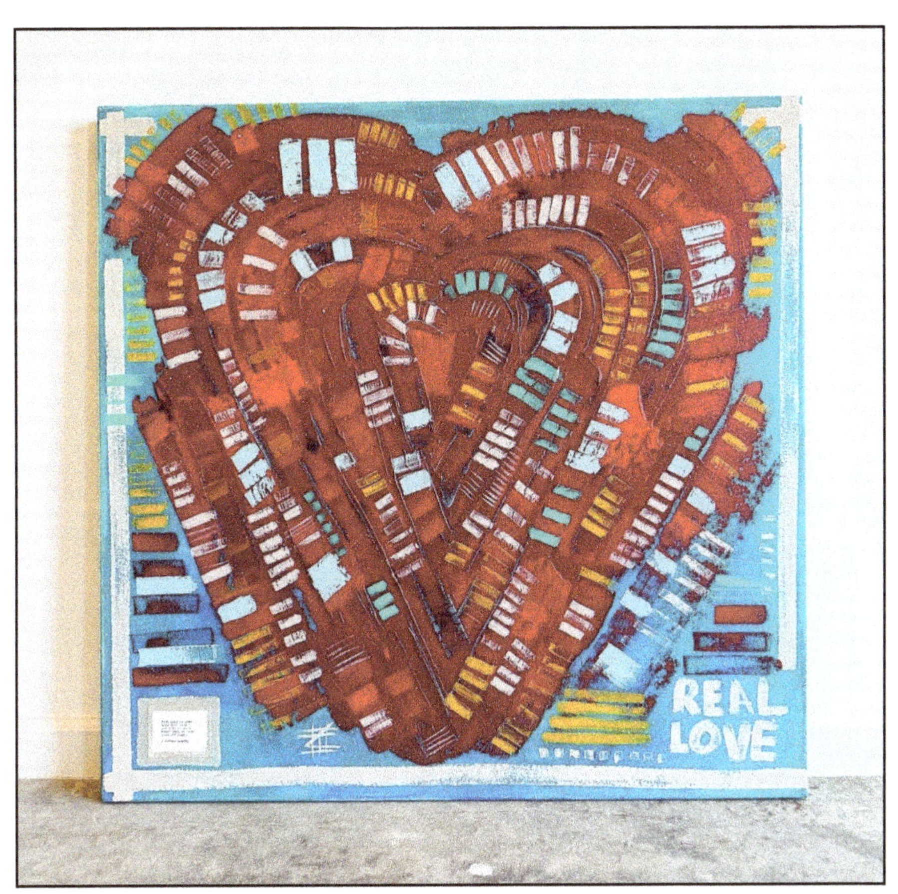
REAL
LOVE

real love is like
a perfect song —
you feel it with
every part of your
body and soul.

/ topher kearby

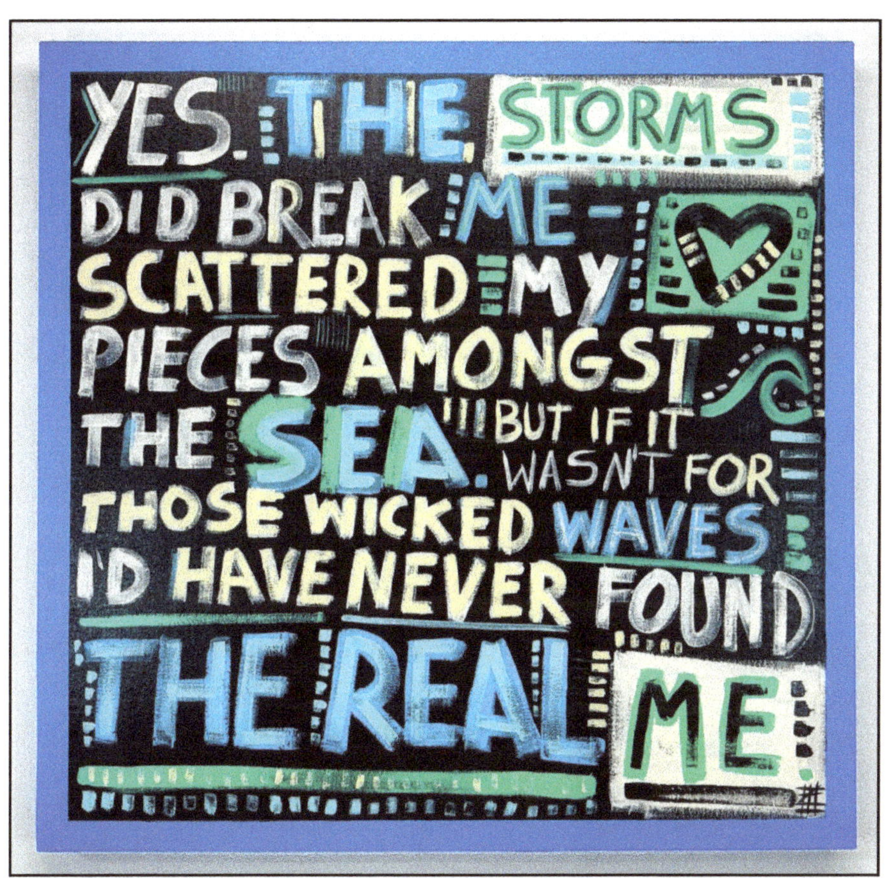

HOPEFUL TRAVELER

what a beautiful thing
it is to be you.

this person whose strength
has been built through the
fires of life.

this spirit that has been
born through joy and
perseverance.

this hope and love that
together have created
a life to be proud of.

celebrate these moments –
you have earned every
ounce of this happiness.

/ topher kearby

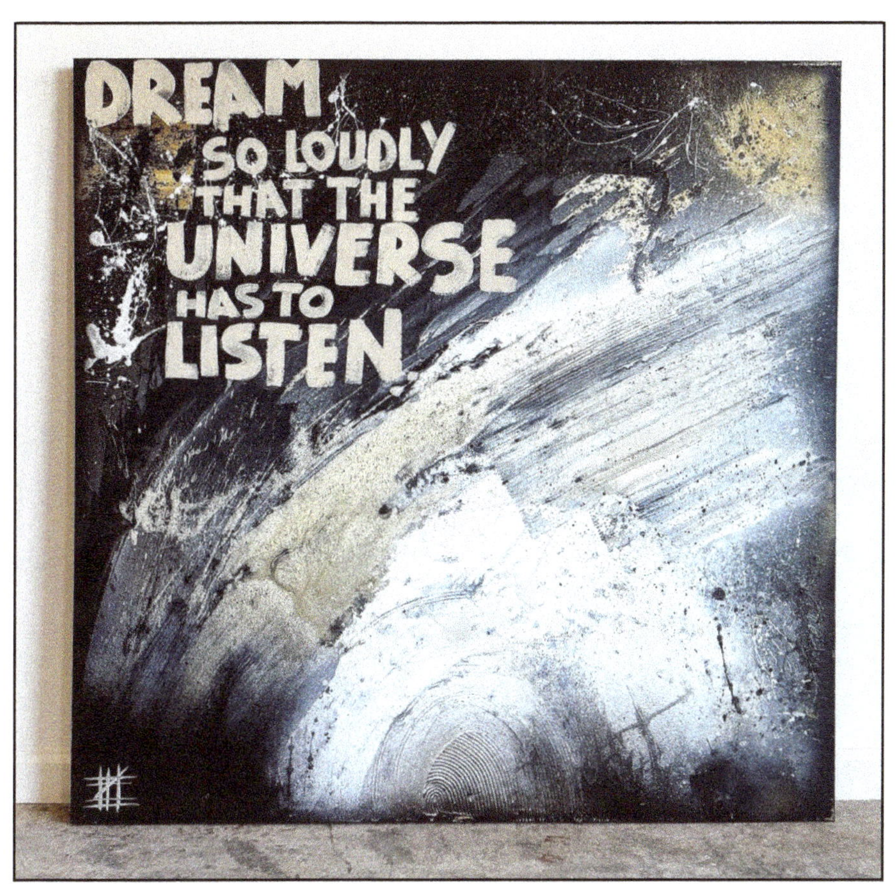

HOPEFUL TRAVELER

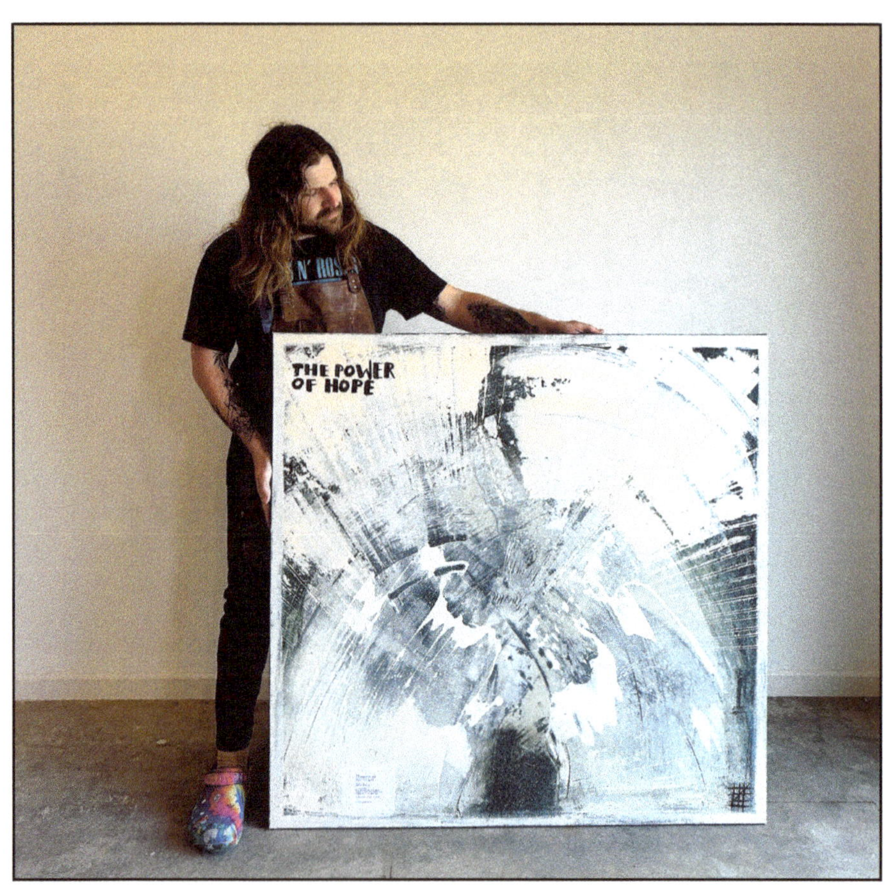

THE POWER
OF HOPE

"come back up for air."

a simple idea that has changed
the way i process difficult times.
no - i don't need to have it all
figured out. or know exactly what
i need to do next. i just need to
breathe and be present.

to take a moment, a minute,
or a month to process what i
need to and remember that i
will not drown or fail if i
need to rest.

i am simply coming back up
for air.

/ topher kearby

i've been many things
in this life. but with
you - i am truly happy.

/ topher kearby

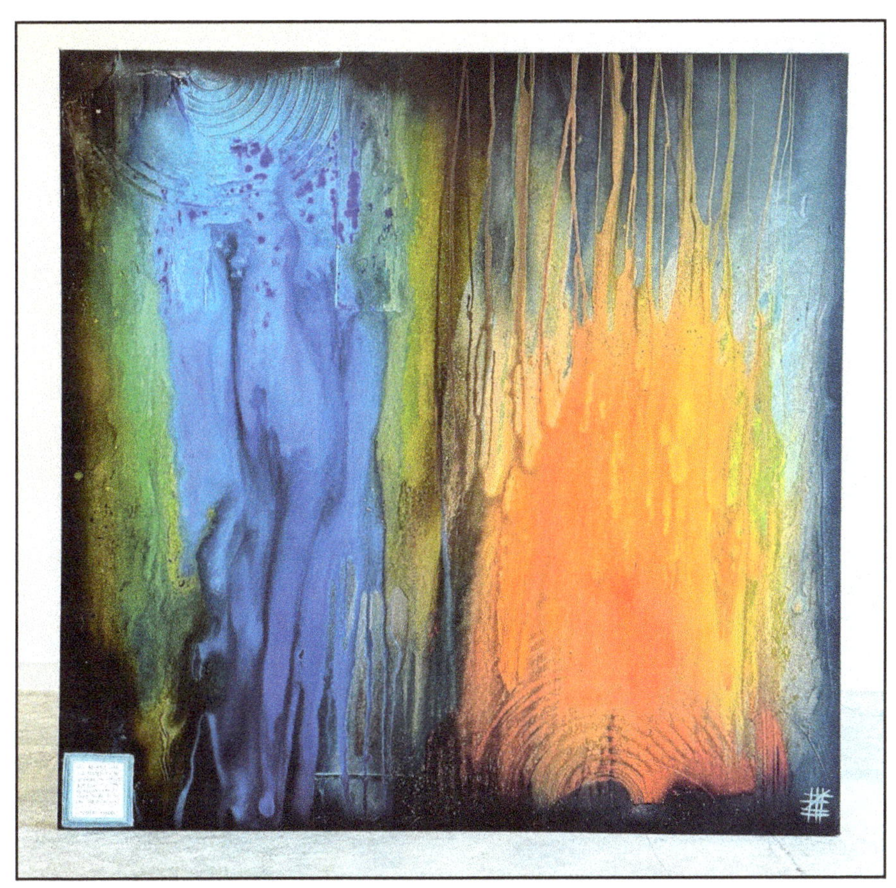

you became who
you needed to be
in order to survive,
but now it's time
to become who you
need to be so you
can thrive in life.

/ topher kearby

i said, "i love you."

but what i meant was —

you are my safe place
in a world that is often
so harsh and difficult
to understand. i am
completely free to be
myself with you. and
that's a feeling i've
not known before.

/ topher kearby

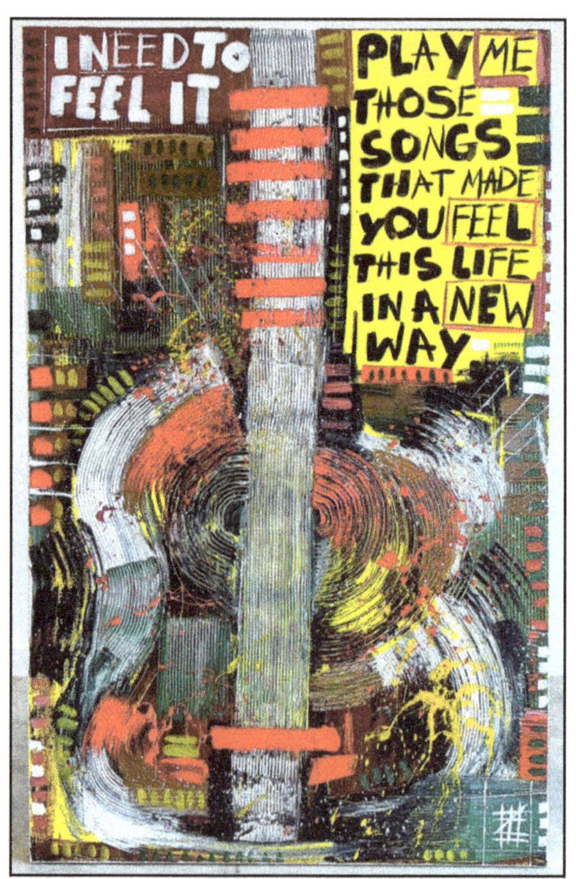

I NEED TO
FEEL IT
PLAY ME
THOSE
SONGS
THAT MADE
YOU FEEL
THIS LIFE
IN A NEW
WAY

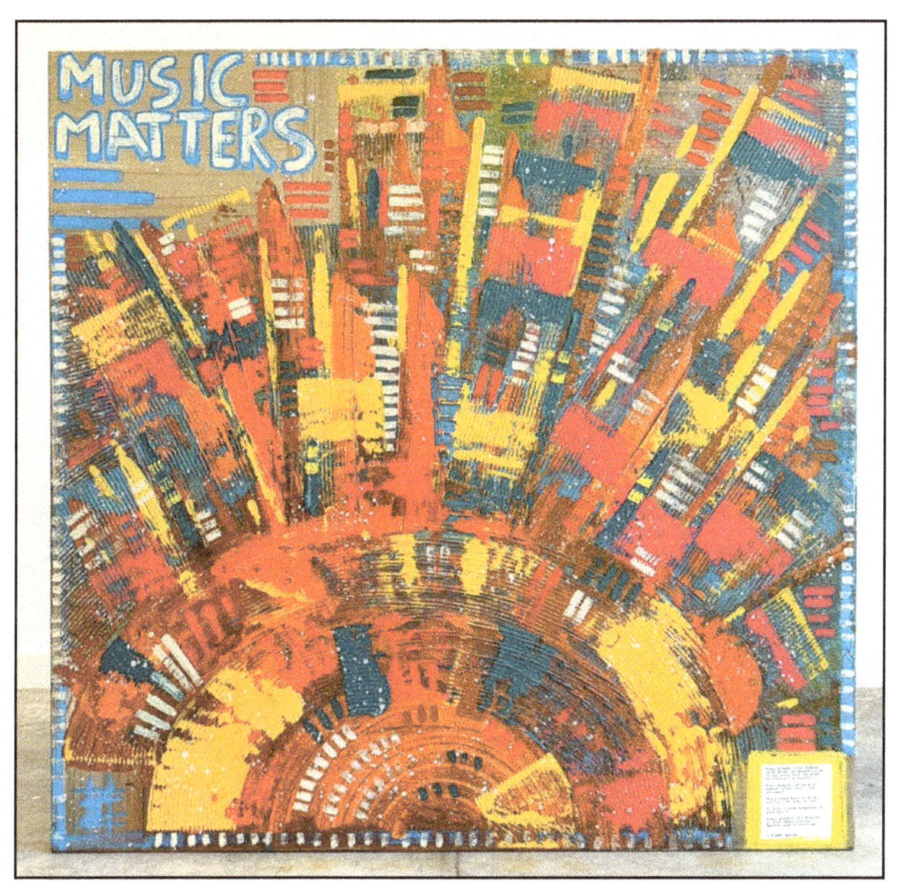
MUSIC
MATTERS

sharing music with someone
is to share the deepest parts
of our souls that are often
so difficult to explain -

"this song helped me know
myself better when i was
younger."

"this album reminds me of
how far i've come in life."

"i fell in love listening to
this band."

music matters. and sharing
it with others creates a
special kind of intimacy.

/ topher kearby

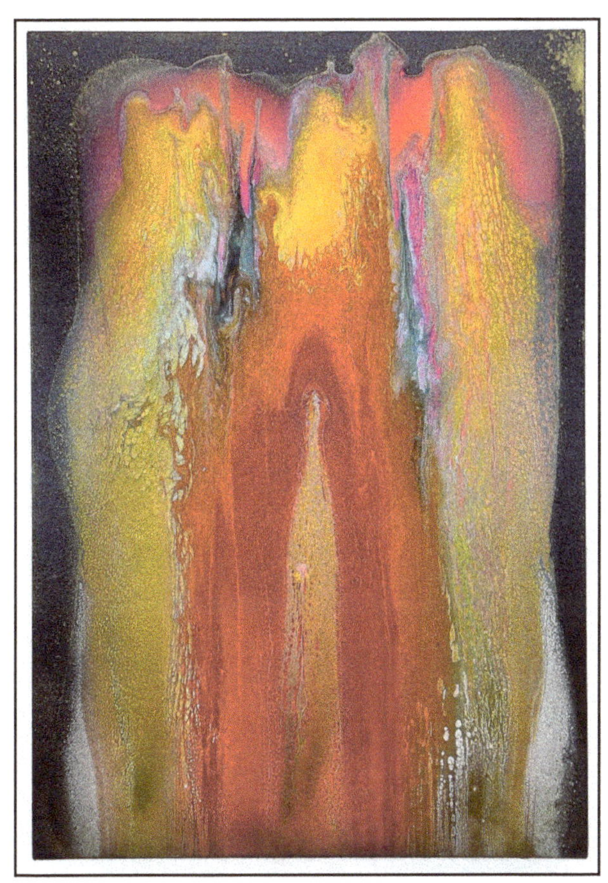

some people make
everything better.
heavy days seem lighter.
dark nights feel brighter.
and it's easier to carry
the weight of it all
when they are around.

/ topher kearby

Who you are may make people
uncomfortable at times.

That's a good thing.

It just means you are here to
help people see the world in a
new way.

Our journeys are unique and to
learn to tell them authentically
is a powerful skill. The more we
hold back our truths the less we
can help others.

"Your story is not my own but
it helped me understand mine
more clearly."

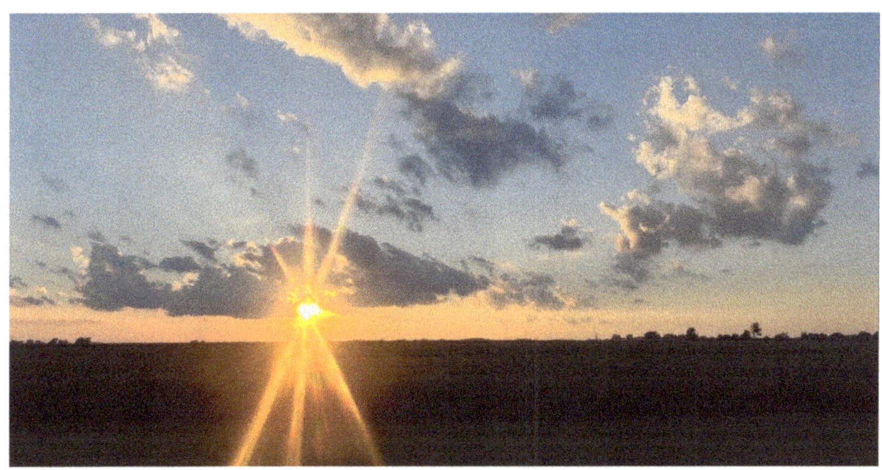

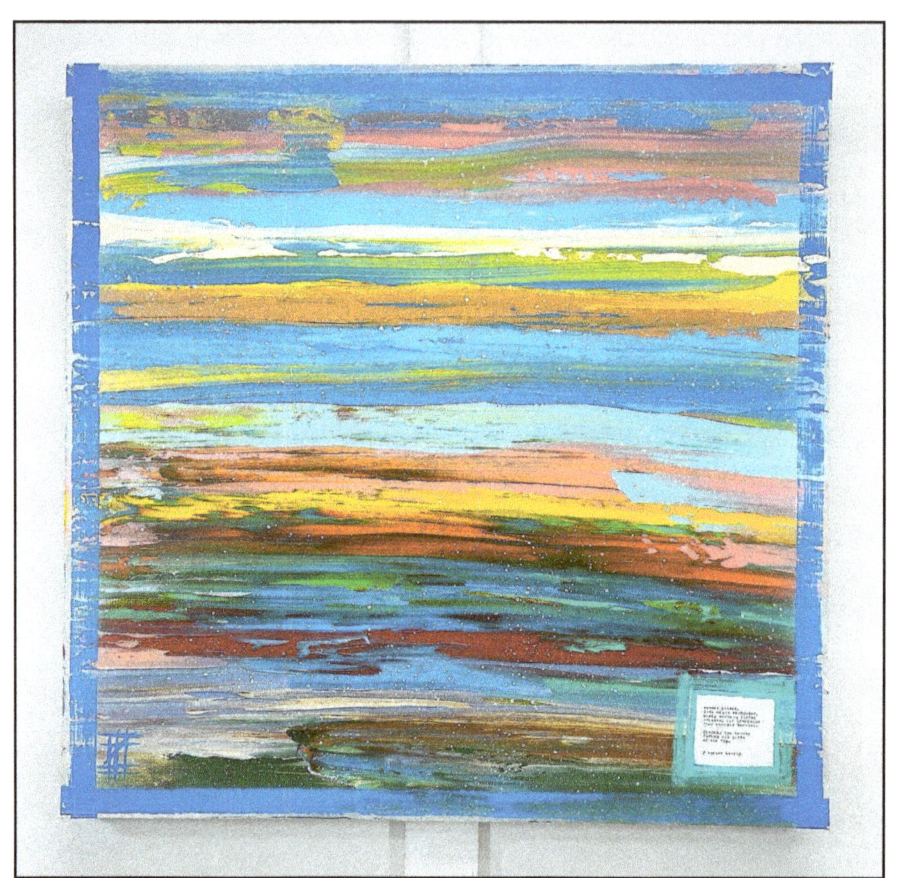

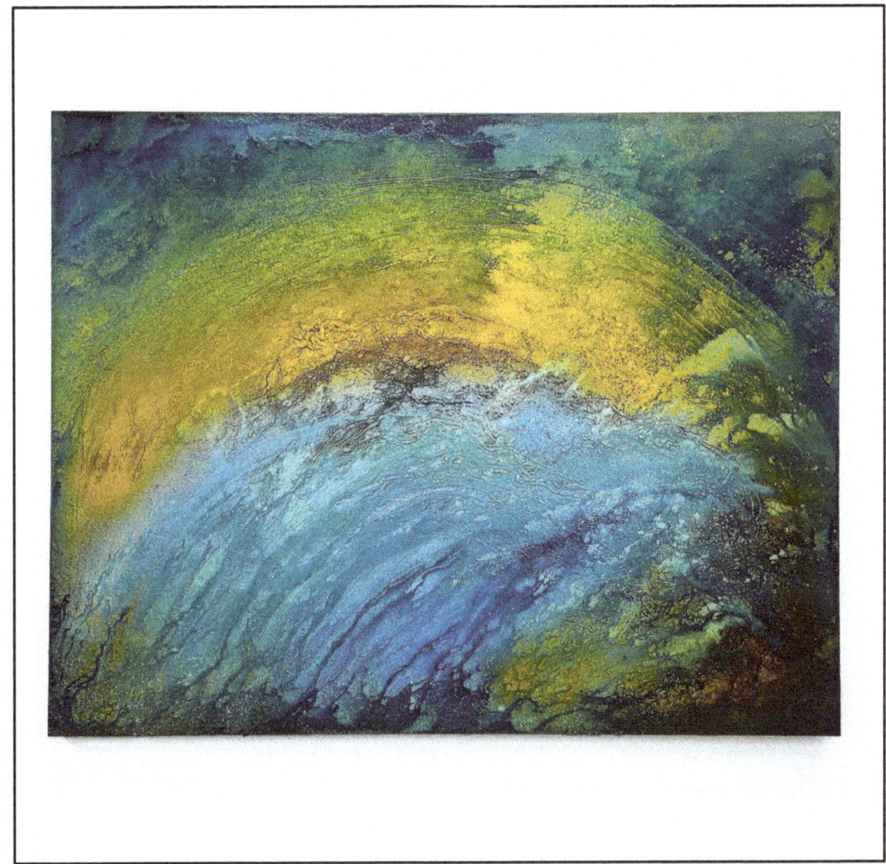

HOPEFUL **TRAVELER**

yes.
the storm did break me.
scattered my pieces
amongst the sea.

but if it weren't for
those wicked waves i'd
have never found the
real me.

/ topher kearby

i just needed a minute.
that's all. a chance to
recharge. remember who
i am. rest isn't a reward.
it's a necessity. and when
you sacrifice peace for
productivity — you end up
being hollowed out.

so listen to your mind,
body, and soul. give them
what they need most —
time to heal.

/ topher kearby

loving ourselves unconditionally
so often means stepping out of
what harms us and moving into
situations that help us grow
and heal.

/ topher kearby

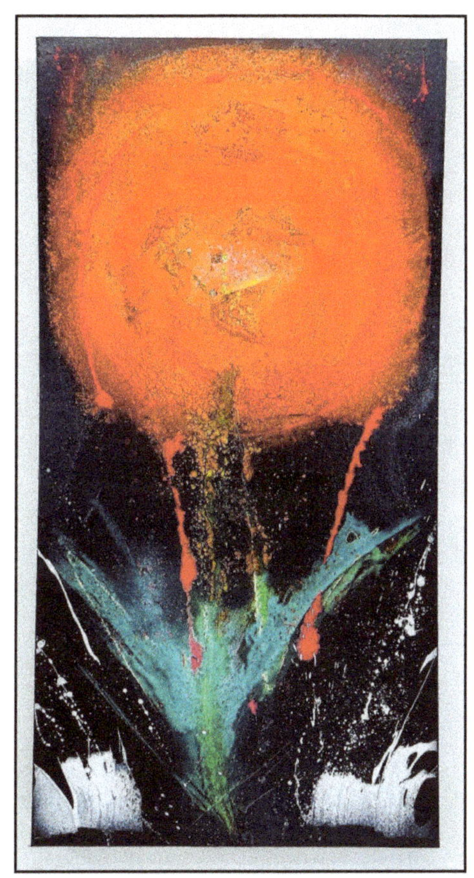

HOPEFUL **TRAVELER**

we are wildflowers —

growing not where we
were planted, but blooming
in the untamed places that
most would never attempt
to reach.

/ topher kearby

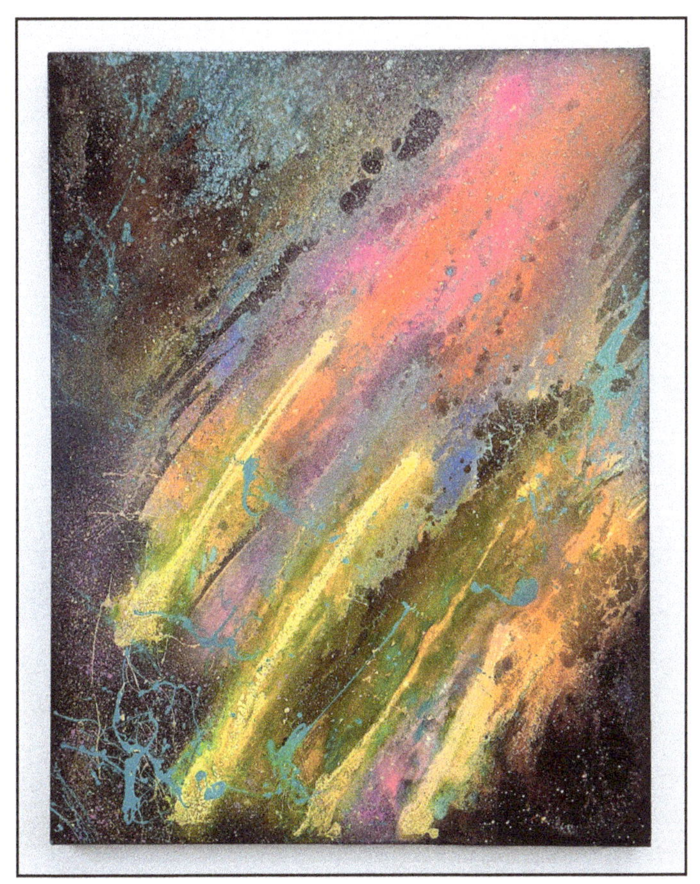

HOPEFUL **TRAVELER**

"I did my best."

That phrase can carry with it so much pressure to do well every moment of every day. But to truly do our best means to be okay with doing more than we planned and also much less that we had hoped.

Our best is what we are able to bring to the table at that moment. And those moments add up to our days.

That is all we have, and it is enough.

Learning that truth was one of the most important lessons of my life. It didn't happen overnight. It wasn't perfect. I simply asked myself at the end of each day, "Did I do my best today?"

And the answer was always, "yes."

Not because I accomplished everything I thought I needed to that day, but because I was present in the moments I lived.

That is the goal of this beautiful life – to be here.

To experience all of it.

The good the bad.

The everything.

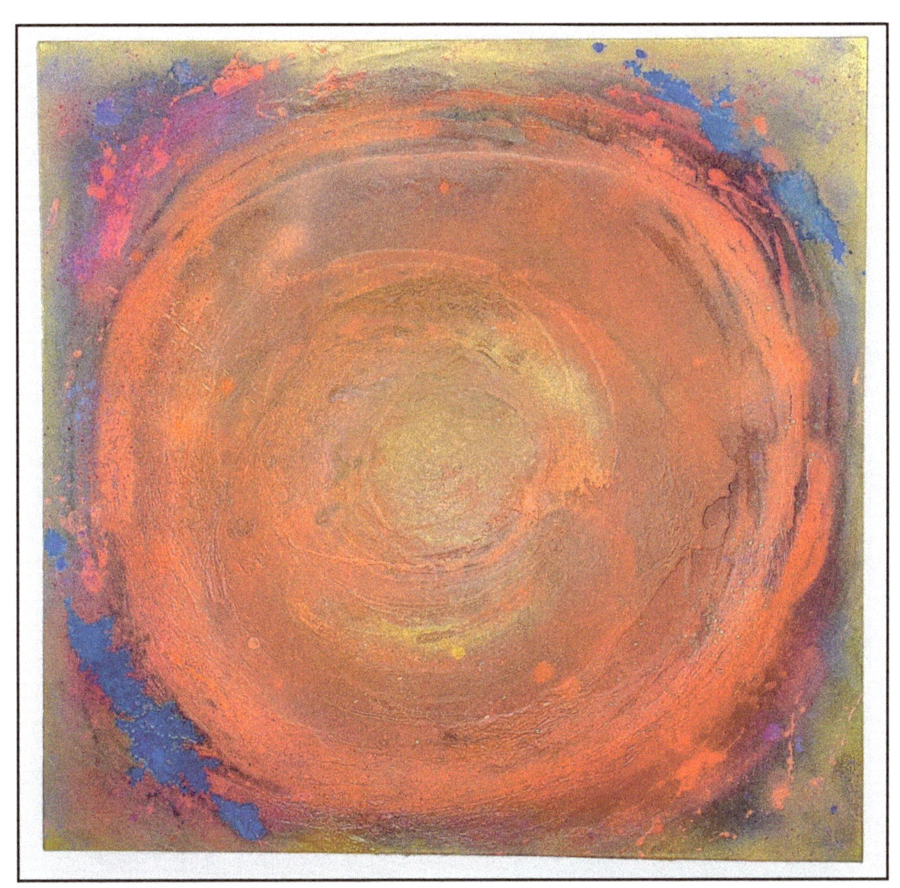

HOPEFUL **TRAVELER**

aren't you ever
worried about
what people
will think?

"i'm too busy
manifesting
the life i am
meant to live."

/ topher kearby

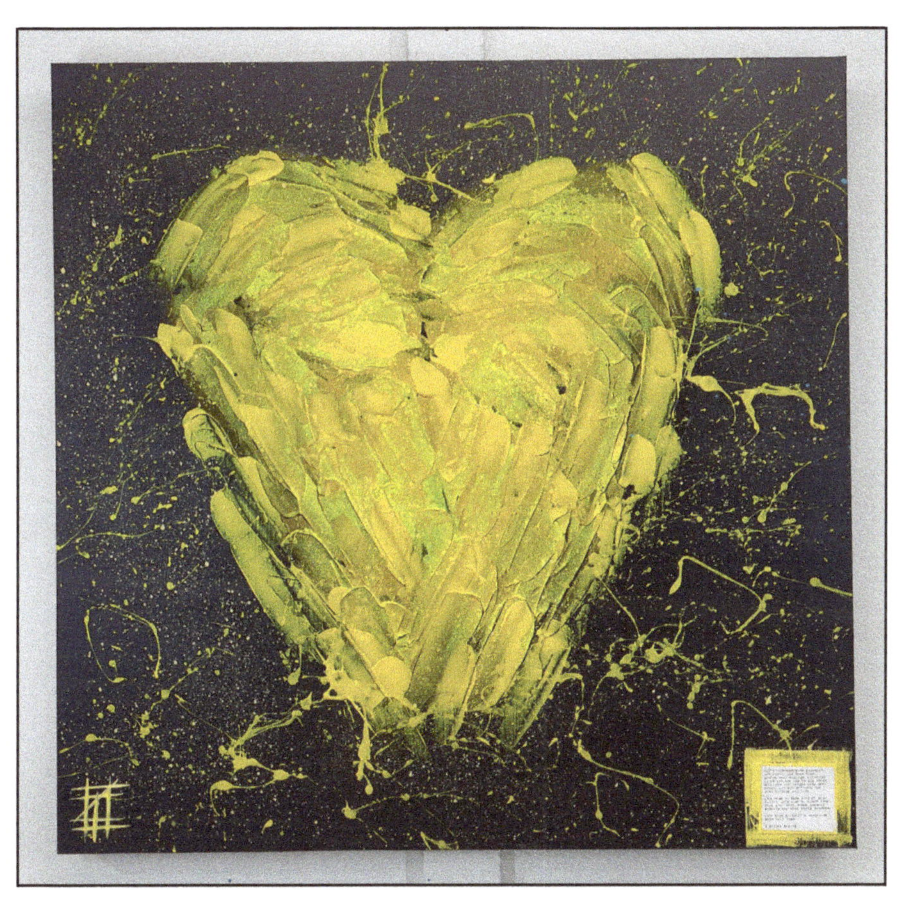

HOPEFUL TRAVELER

don't underestimate yourself.
not again. not this time.
you've been through the worst
of it and are now on the other
side. the challenges have been
tough. but you met each one
with courage and love.

it's time to take hold of your
future. it's time to break free
from your past. these present
moments are what truly matters.

it's time to build a happiness
that will last.

/ topher kearby

spend as much time doing
what you love with the
people you love -

that's the path toward
lasting happiness.

/ topher kearby

the light within us
shines so brightly when
we focus it towards the
places our hearts long
to go.

/ topher kearby

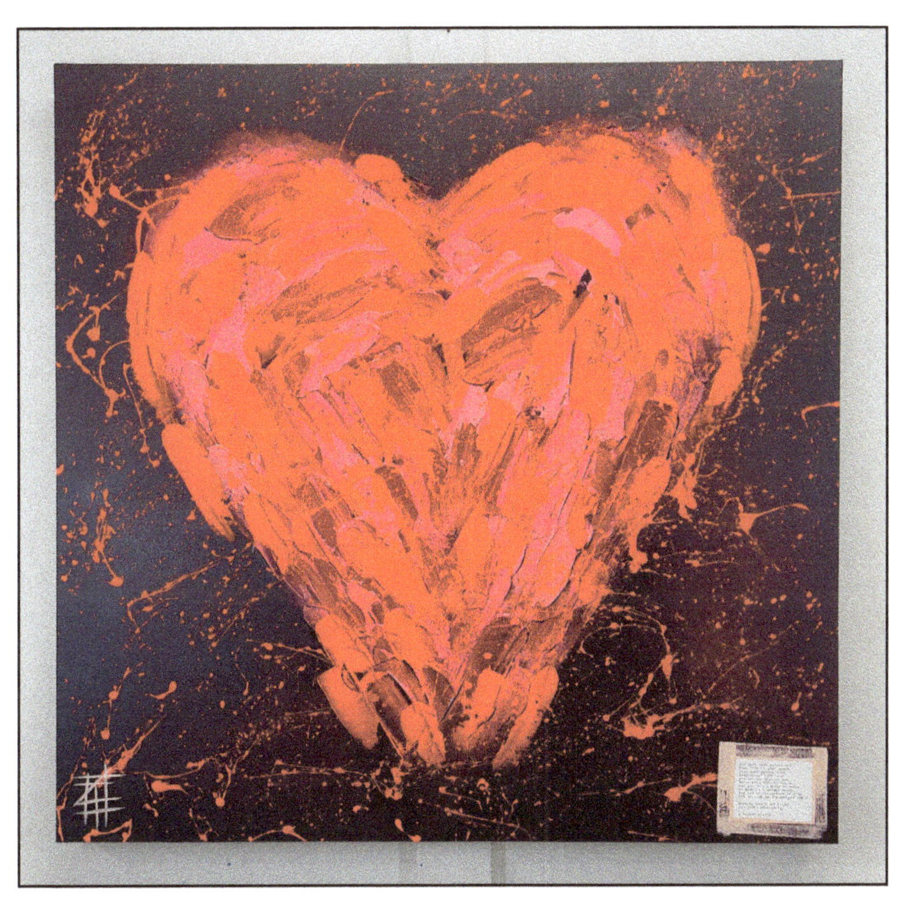

you were born with a bit
more fire in your heart
than most people. it's
passion and it's love.
you see the best in the
world even when it hurts.
and you do whatever it takes
to make it a better place.
not out of obligation or pity.
but because that's who you are —

someone who live fully
and loves completely.

/ topher kearby

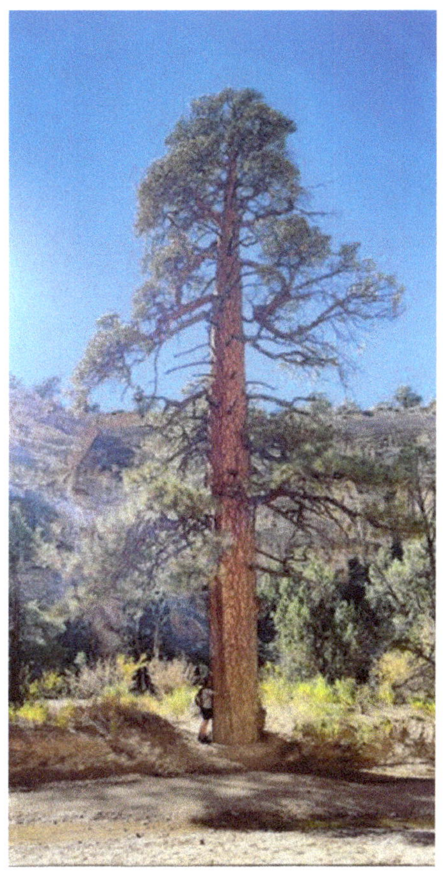

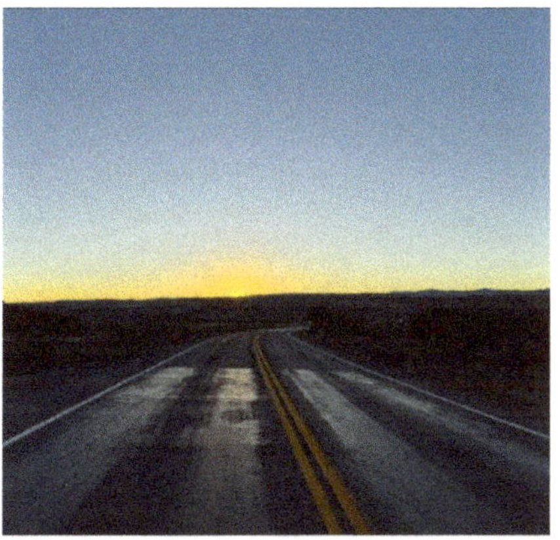

treasure your friendships.

the family you were not born into, but the one that often knows you best. they love you not because they have to, but because their lives wouldn't be the same without you. and you feel the same about them.

that closeness and that bond should be treasured. because life becomes so much more full and beautiful when you share it with true friends.

/ topher kearby

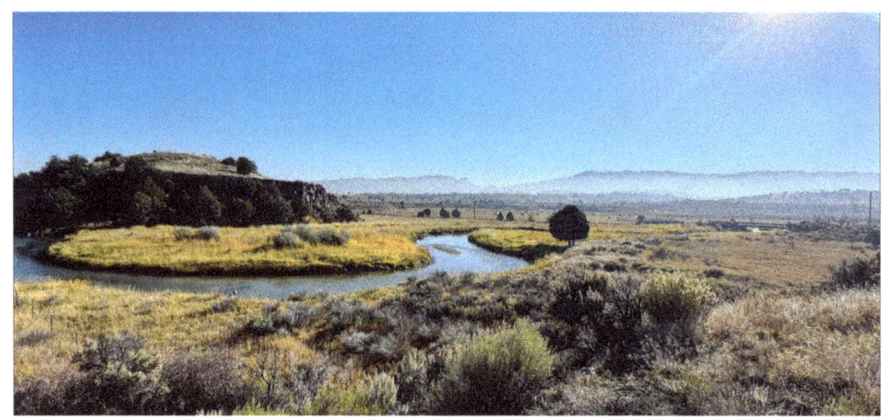

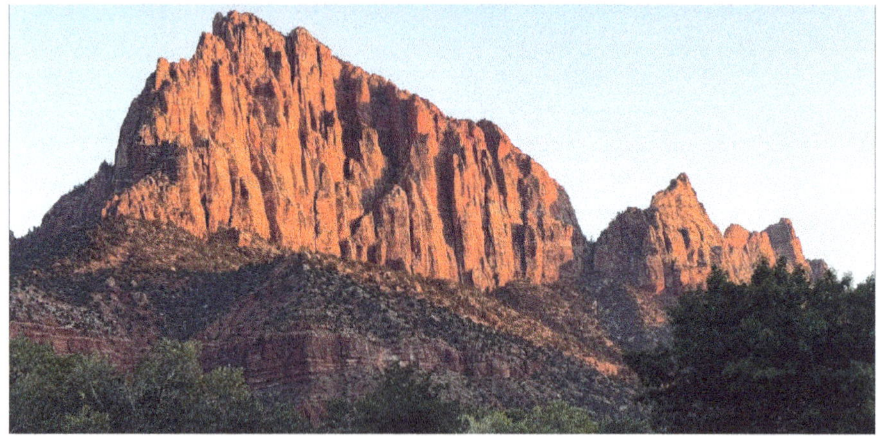

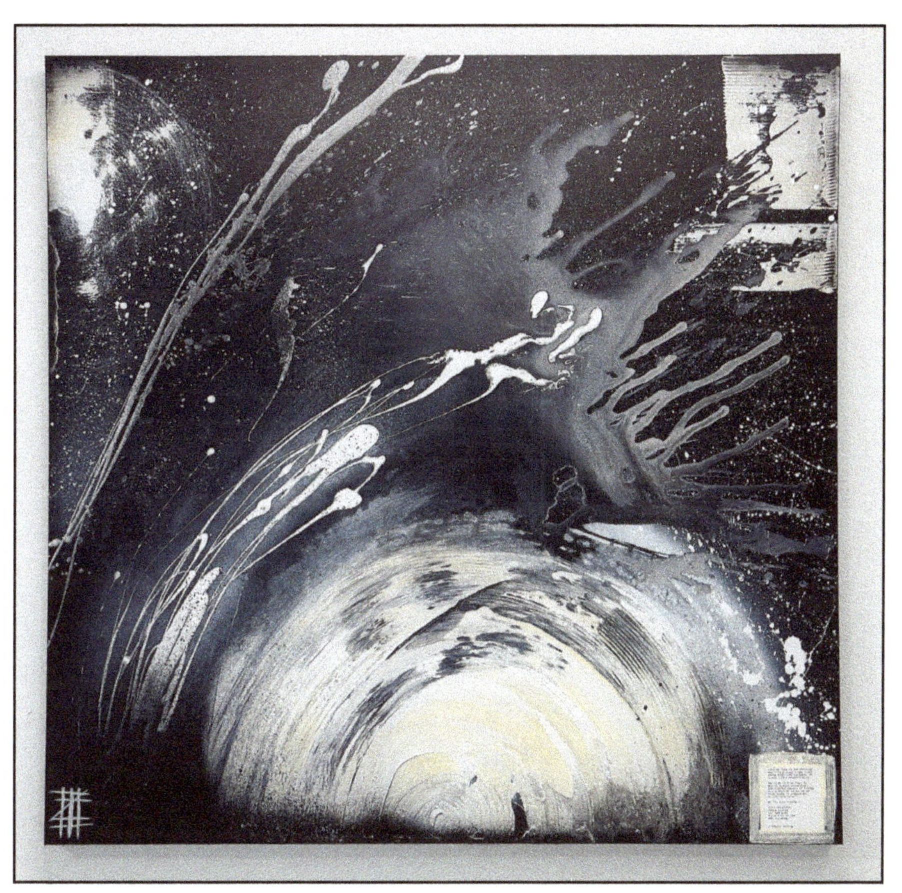

HOPEFUL **TRAVELER**

when we look at the evening
sky long enough, a few dozen
stars turn into an ocean of
light – it's breathtaking.

the same is true when we
search within ourselves.
the limited amount of energy
and potential we think we
have pales in comparison
to our true fire.

so don't hold back –

burn brightly, dream loudly,
and let your voice echo
across the universe.

/ topher kearby

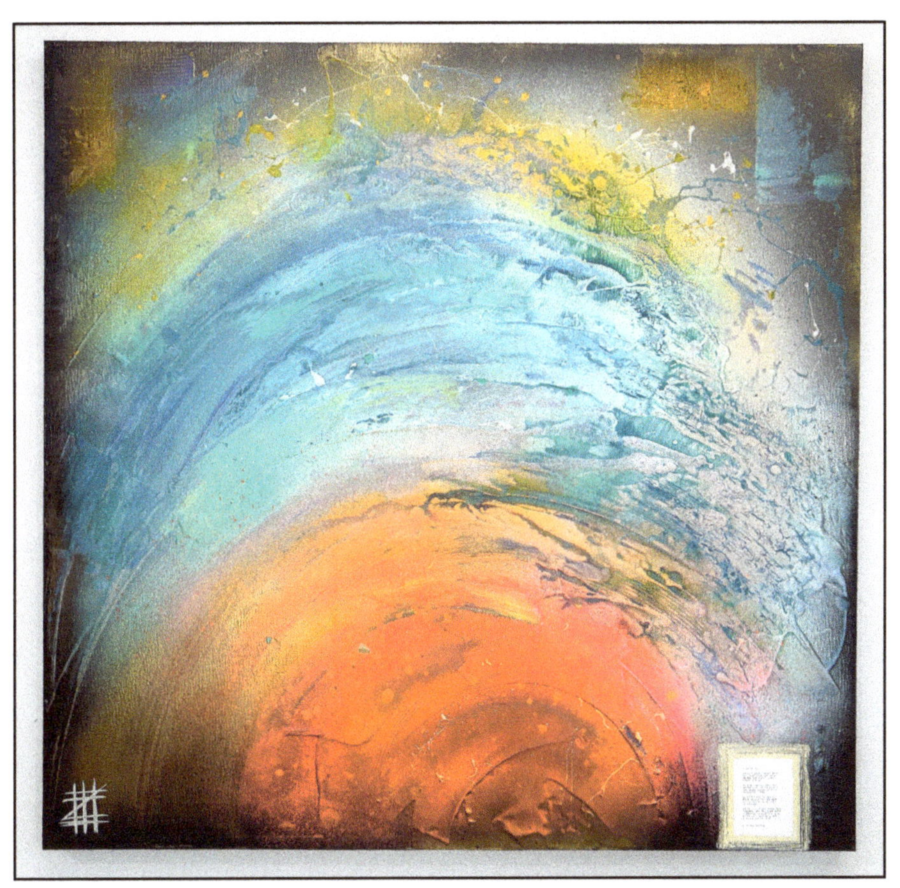

i am ready —

to have experiences that
are inspiring and help
me see the world with
fresh vision.

to lay down my need for
perfection and embrace
the messy parts of this
beautiful life.

to watch the sunset and
know that i did my best
today and that my best
is enough.

to be a wild and wonderful
dreamer. who believes that
anything is possible with
a bit of creativity and a
whole lot of love.

/ topher kearby

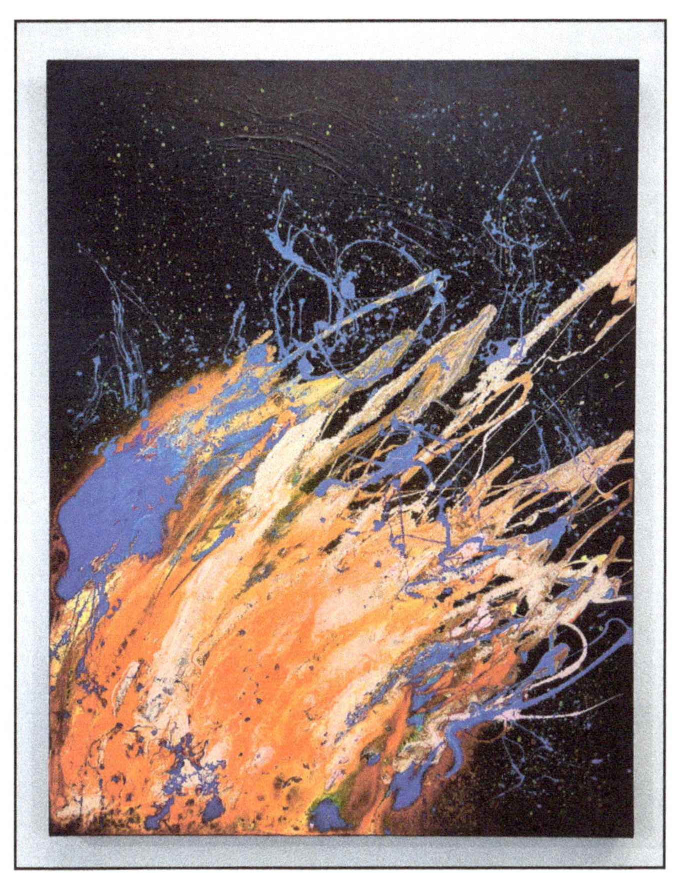

The experiences that shape us are rarely the ones that we would ever choose to live through.

They are often difficult, painful, and downright impossible to survive. And that's just what we do during those times – survive.

We grit our teeth, toughen up in ways we have to, and push through until things finally get better.

It's exhausting.

But it doesn't last forever.

We eventually get to the other side of the pain. The long night slips away and becomes a bright morning sky full of hope and possibilities. We feel refreshed and renewed. As if anything is possible.

But it's hard to remember that it gets better during times of grief or sorrow.

It's easy to see the sunrise and be filled with hope, but it's difficult to remember that there will be a sunrise when we are in the midst of a period of darkness.

But a new day will rise.

We just need to believe it.

understanding who you are
and what you want out of
life is the path toward
real happiness.

it takes time.
it takes effort.
but the rewards is a life
that is both fulfilling
and uniquely yours.

/ topher kearby

love is celebrating joy.
sharing pain. understanding
more deeply what it means to
be human. to be beautifully
imperfect. to be wonderfully
lost at times.

to share stories and make
new memories - together.

that is real life.
that is real love.

/ topher kearby

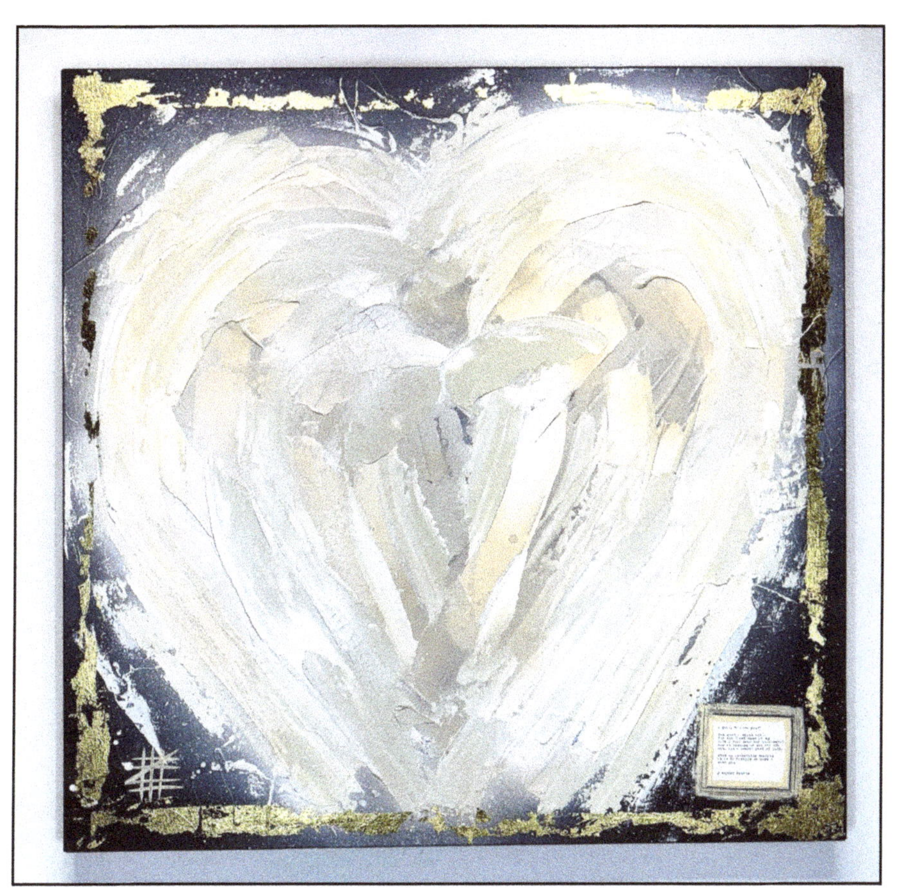

HOPEFUL TRAVELER

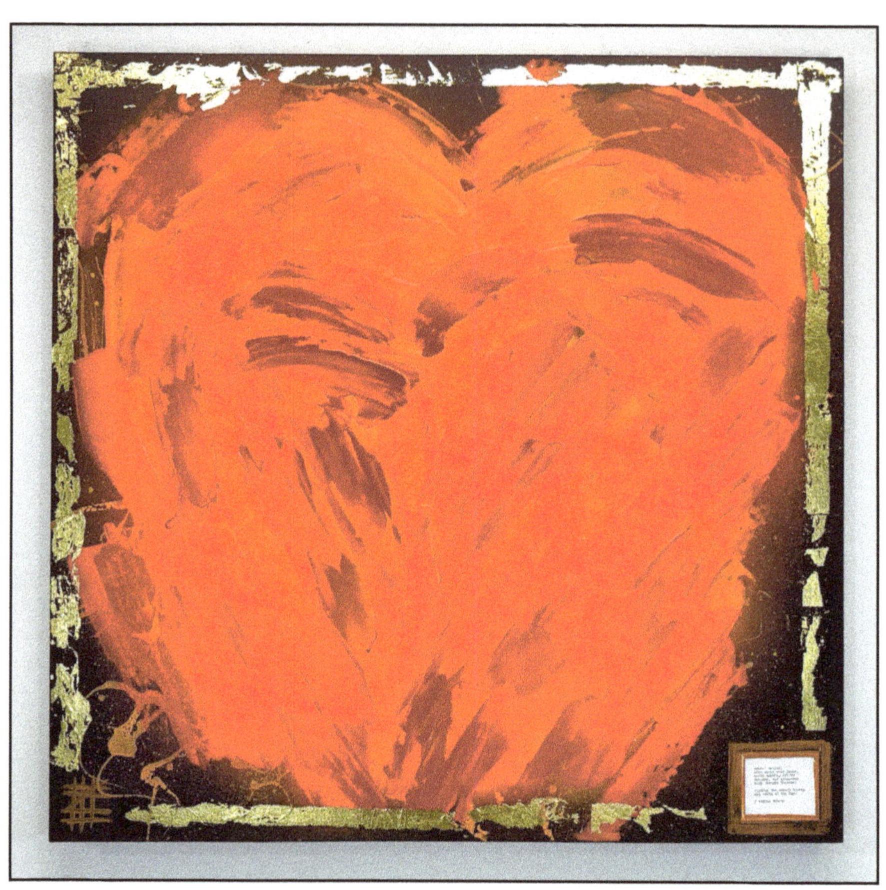

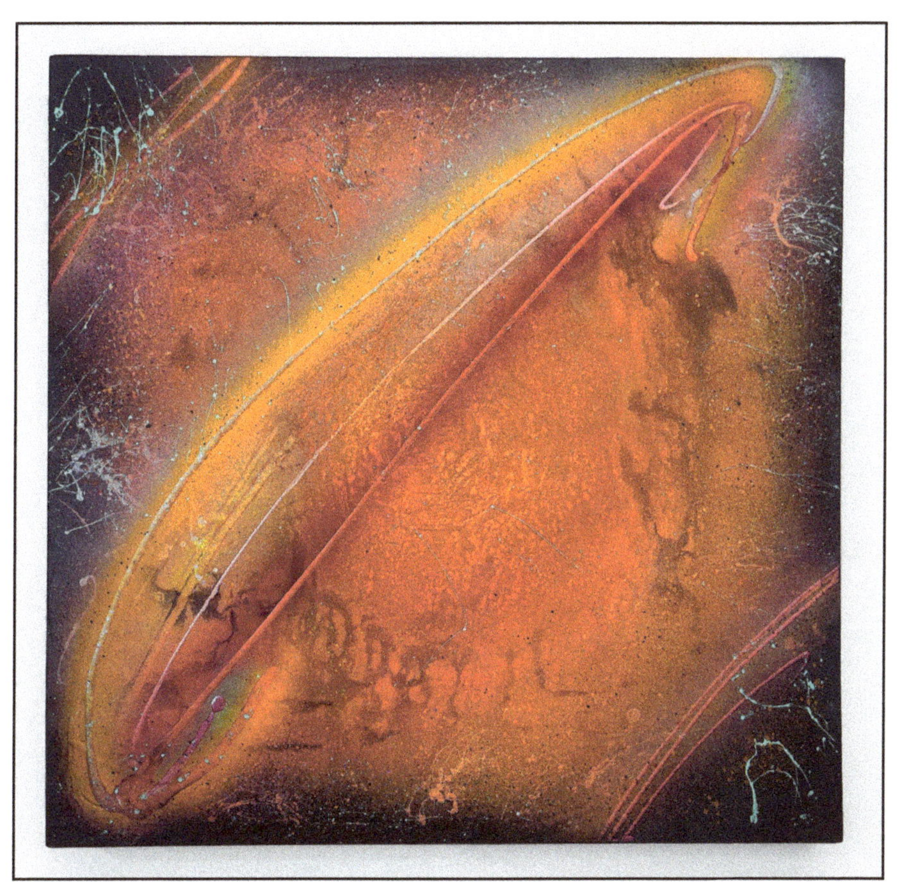

HOPEFUL TRAVELER

not everyone will understand
your passion, your joy, your
love, or your purpose.

that's just fine.
fitting in only works if you
shave off enough of yourself
to squeeze into other people's
expectations. you do that
long enough and there will
be barely anything left of
the real you.

instead, let your spirit shake
the mountains. step into your
full power by learning to love
every ounce of your fire.

/ topher kearby

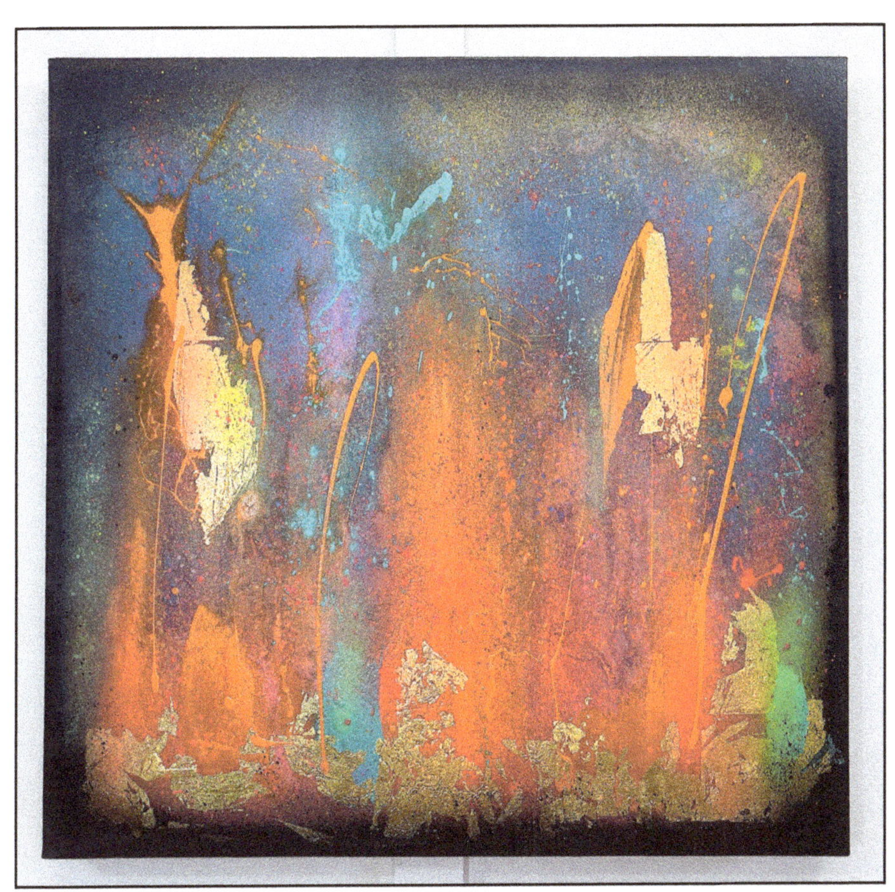

HOPEFUL **TRAVELER**

Hope isn't an easy answer to life's trials – it's a tool to help us find purpose through our pain.

Think of all of your experiences, the good and the bad, as tools in your tool bag. Each one teaches us something that we can use in life.

Often in ways that we wouldn't expect.

Some of those lessons are for us. They show us what we are capable of accomplishing, where our strengths are, and how to use our talents to get where we need to go in life.

Some lessons are given to us so we can help others. It can be simply sharing a resource, giving guidance, or being the example of what life looks like on the other side of the darkness.

We each have unique experiences but so many of us feel alone because we are afraid to say, "I understand a bit of what you are going through because I have lived through something similar. It wasn't easy but I made it through. I'm here when you need me."

That kind of vulnerability saves lives.

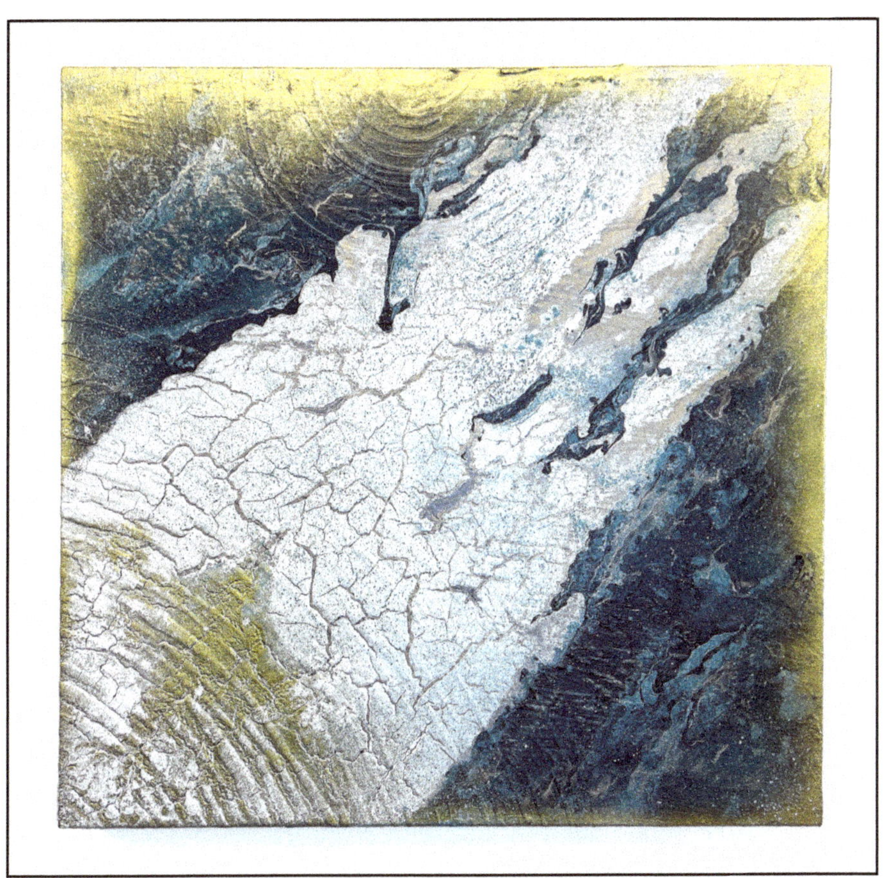

HOPEFUL **TRAVELER**

be someone who isn't
afraid to take risks.
who sees life as an
adventure. who wakes
up on a new day and
says, "i may not know
what life has planned
for me, but i know i'll
be ready."

embrace the unknown.
follow your heart.
and learn just how
strong you are along
the way.

/ topher kearby

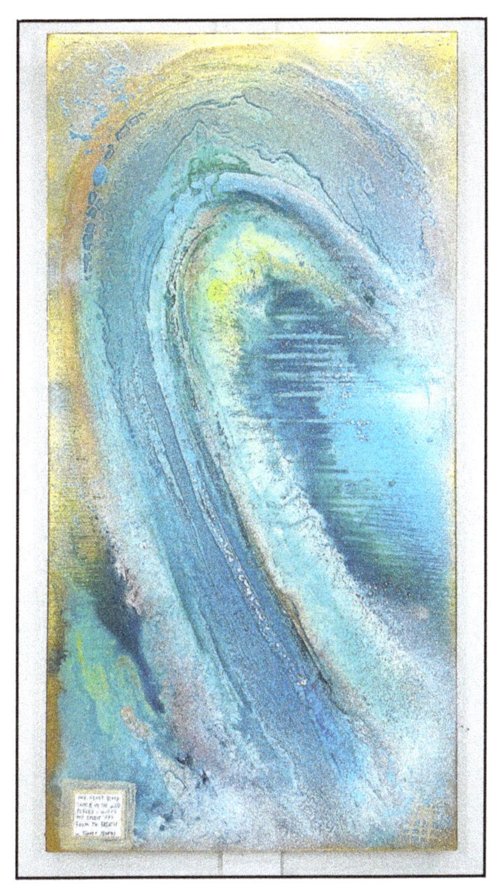

my heart beats
louder in the wild
places —where
my spirit has
room to breathe.

/ topher kearby

everything is different now.

change has moved in so gently
that you barely noticed. but
the world feels brighter.

and life feels lighter.

who you were seems like a
distant memory. because who
you are now is someone who is
no longer content to survive.

everything is different;
and so are you.

it's time to make the most of
this life –

it's time to thrive.

/ topher kearby

there are some connections
that we cannot explain but
we feel them with every ounce
of our souls –

they change us, shape us,
and help us grow into the
people we are meant to be.

/ topher kearby

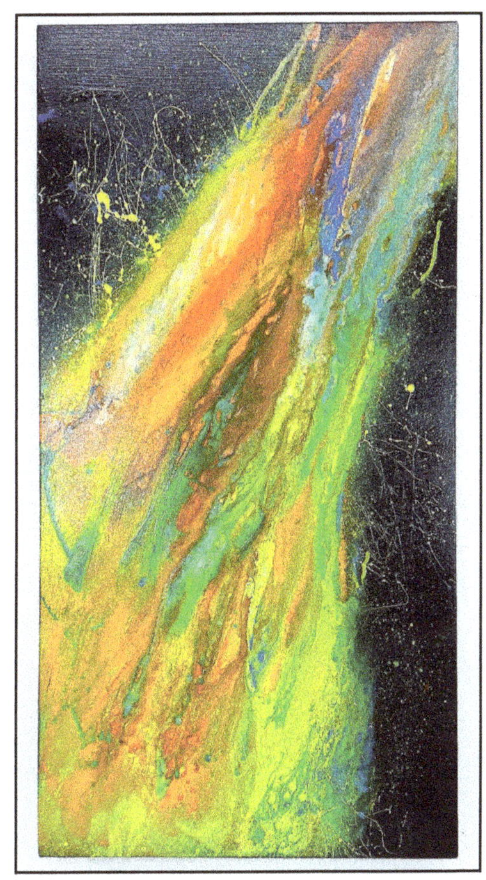

i love journeys that take
me to places where i have
never been.

i love music that makes me
feel in ways that i have
never felt.

and i love people who help
me see the world in ways
that i never expected.

/ topher kearby

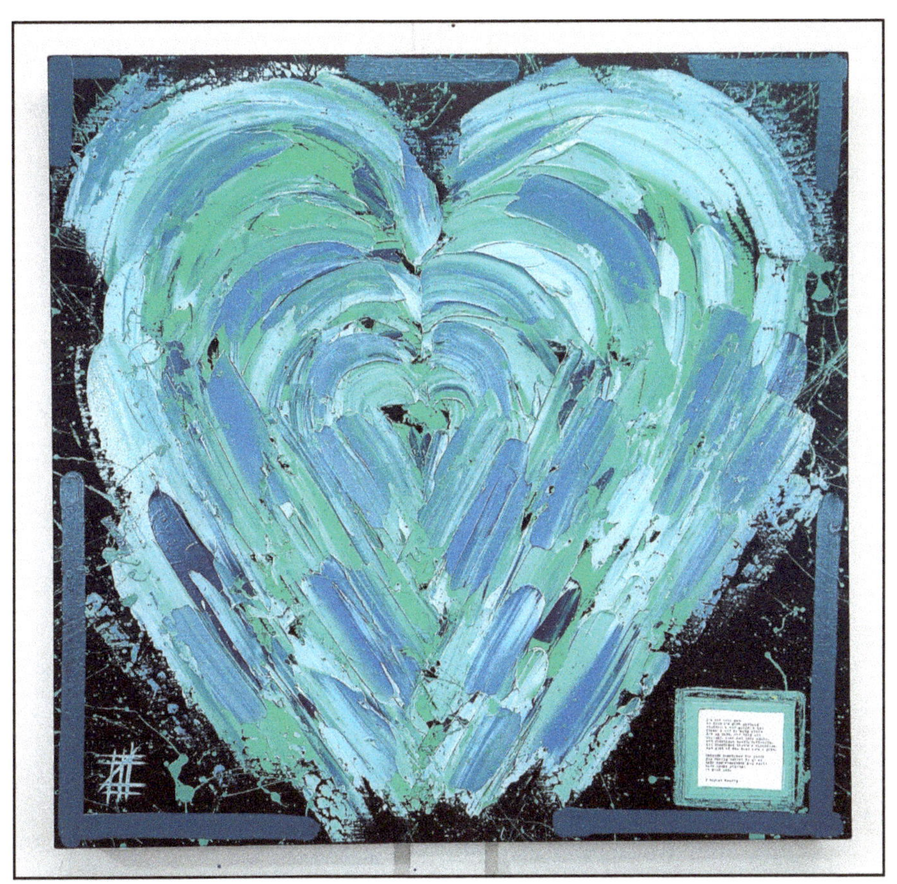

i'm not done yet.
in fact i'm just getting
started. i had goals. i had
ideas. i had so many plans
for my life. and they all
changed. over and over again.
and sometimes that's difficult.
and sometimes that's a challenge.
but most of the time it's a gift.

because sometimes the place
you really needed to go in
life was somewhere you would
have never planned
on your own.

/ topher kearby

through witnessing the
beauty of the "every day"
moments that are so easy
to miss —

we understand that life
is so much more than just
the "big events."

/ topher kearby

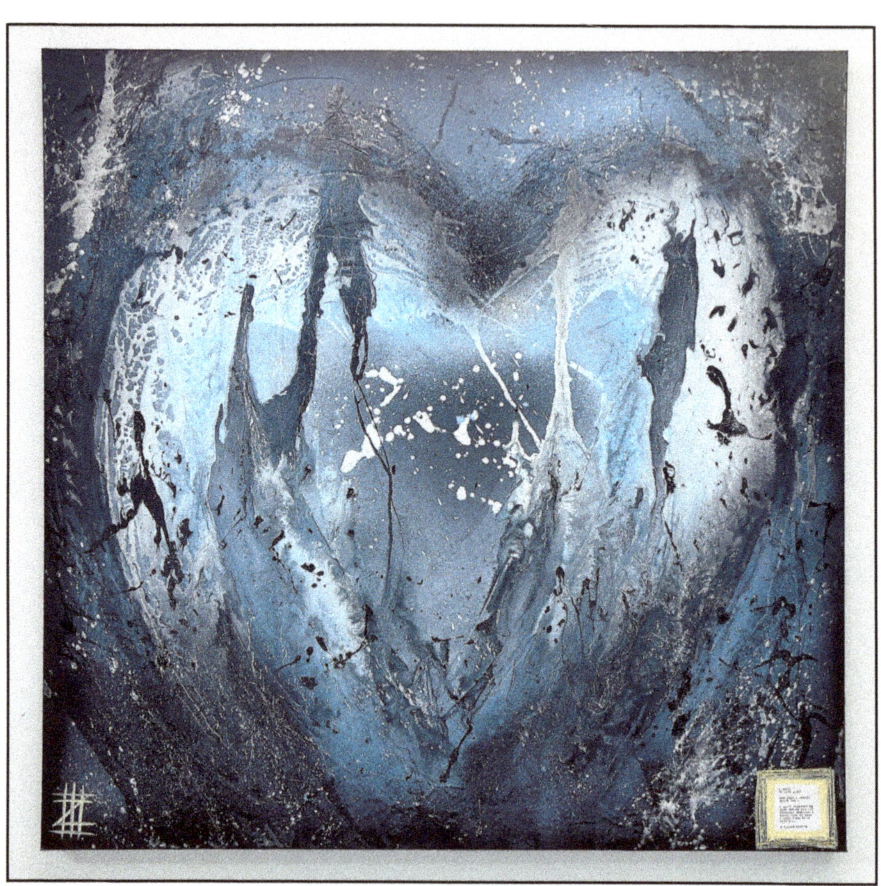

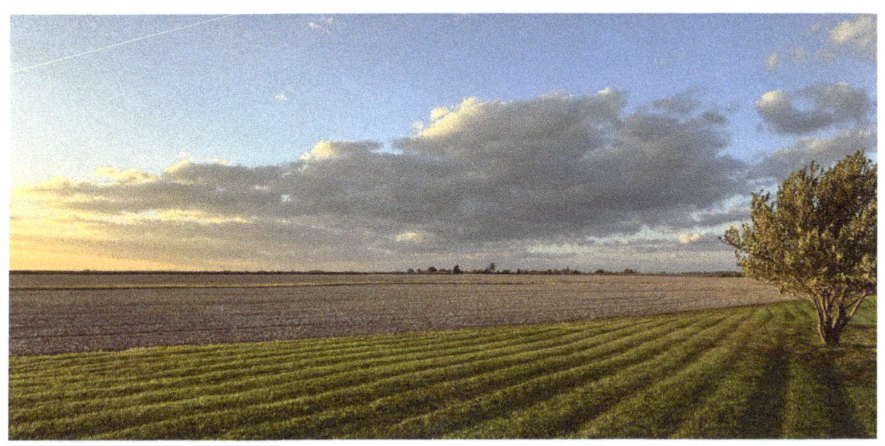

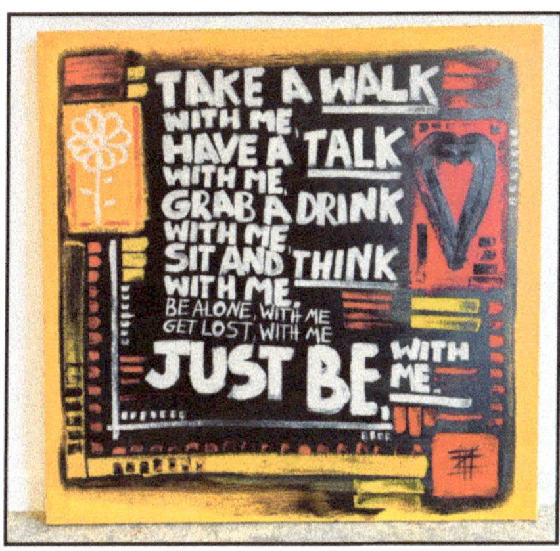

TAKE A WALK
WITH ME,
HAVE A TALK
WITH ME,
GRAB A DRINK
WITH ME
SIT AND THINK
WITH ME.
BE ALONE, WITH ME
GET LOST, WITH ME
JUST BE. WITH ME.

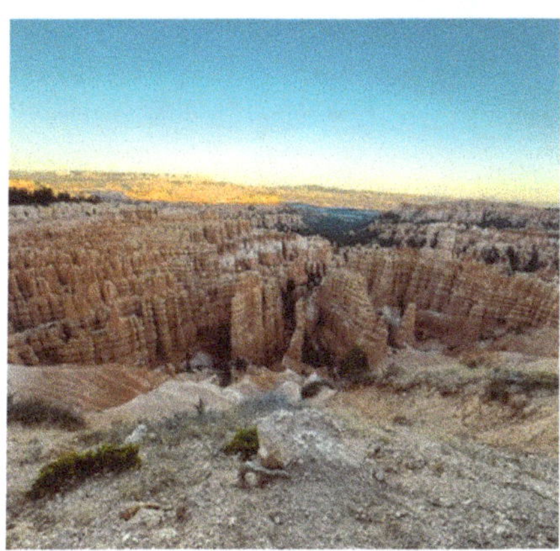

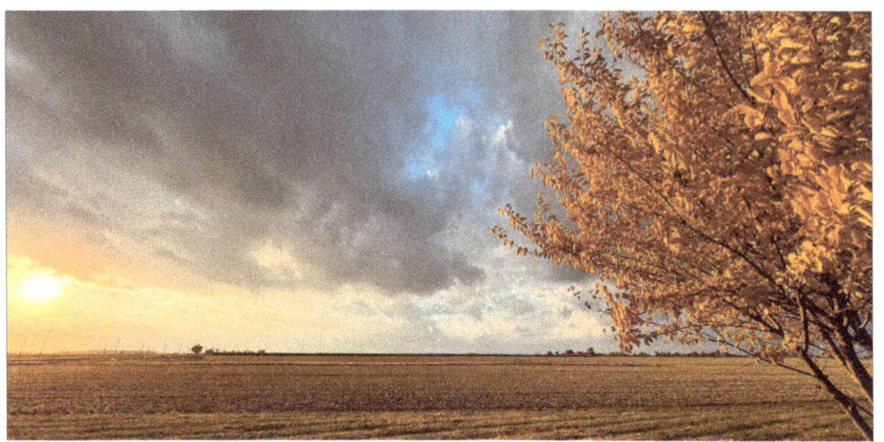

The seasons change and so do we. Nature teaches us so much if we stop and witness.

The leaves fall, the winds howl, and everything is born again.

We move through this life with every ounce of beauty and fire that are contained in the stars,

The night shines – yes.

But so do we.

Let's not waste these moments in front of us waiting for the next big event. It's only now we are given and it's now that we need to live –

Fully and wildly.

With passion and grace that knows no end because within us there is energy that has no limit. We are the captains of our destiny – so let's sail on.

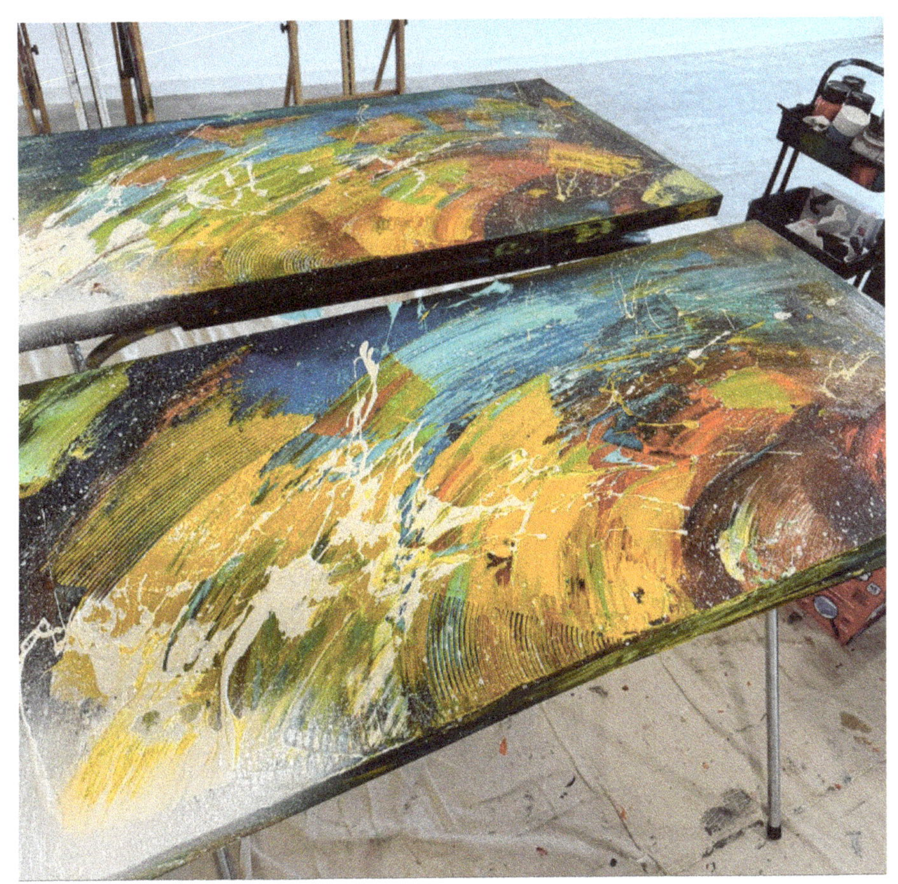

HOPEFUL **TRAVELER**

i'm so thankful for you.
you pushed through the difficult
moments so i can live a full life
on the other side.

i'm so grateful for you.
you stayed true to yourself even
when it felt like the whole world
didn't understand you.

i'm so proud of you.
i wouldn't be the person i am
today without all the sacrifices
you made.

i have so much love for you.
and i still carry your dreams
with me today.

/ topher kearby

yes, we will get to
where we need to go
in life. but it probably
won't be the way we
planned to get there.

after all –it's about
the journey. so, let's
enjoy the detours.

/ topher kearby

"you were there for me."

is the most honest
love story ever told.

/ topher kearby

never underestimate
your ability to turn
an impossible situation
into an experience that
helps you grow.

/ topher kearby

that thunder in your heart
is there for a reason. that
lightning in your mind is
meant to spark you to move
in the direction you're meant
to go. those deep callings
within you are why you are
here — listen to them.

take those risks and make
those changes you're ready
to make. your future begins
today — claim it.

/ topher kearby

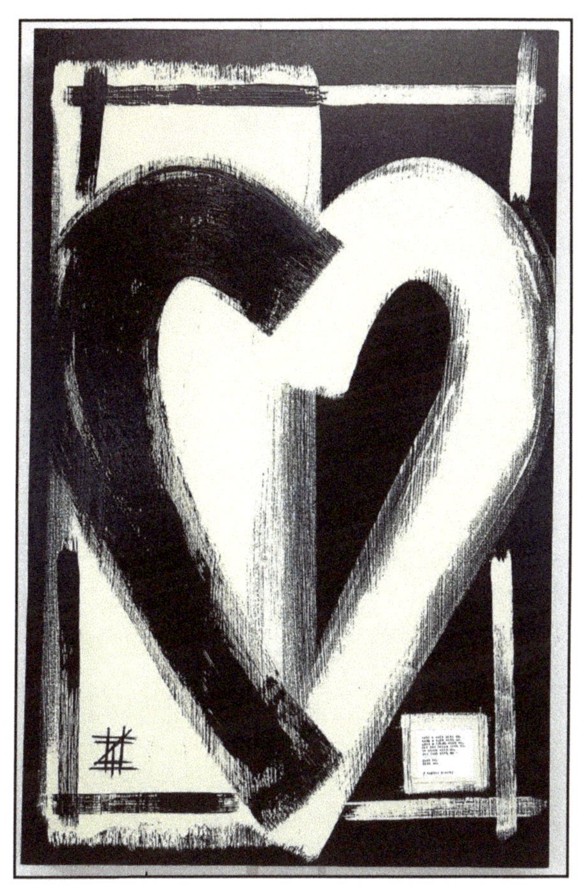

HOPEFUL TRAVELER

Life can feel like a solitary endeavor even when we are surrounded by other people – sometimes, even more so.

That feeling comes from a lack of connection.

We want to be seen, heard, and understood. To be recognized for who we really are and to have our stories be respected. But that takes a level of openness that is difficult to achieve.

Why? Because we all have been in situations where we showed up with our full selves and were rejected. We opened our hearts and instead of being shown love, we were taken advantage of.

It's hard to recover from those experiences.

There is no timeline on healing or forgiveness.

So, we often wall up and stay safe instead of being vulnerable enough to help others. That's understandable. Everyone has the right to do what they need to do to survive.

But once we are ready to connect with others, we unlock our true power – love.

don't quit. don't give up.
don't dull your shine just
because it makes people
uncomfortable. who you are
is important. what you bring
to this world is needed. that
fire. that passion. that heart
that beats so powerfully
inside your chest.

that's the good stuff.
go after it.

/ topher kearby

we are connected —
as the waves are
to the oceans and
the stars are to
the seas.

i no longer fear
what tomorrow brings
because i know that
through it all you
will be with me.

/ topher kearby

let your passions
and your purpose
echo so loudly that
the universe has no
choice but to respond,

"i hear you, i see you,
and you're ready."

/ topher kearby

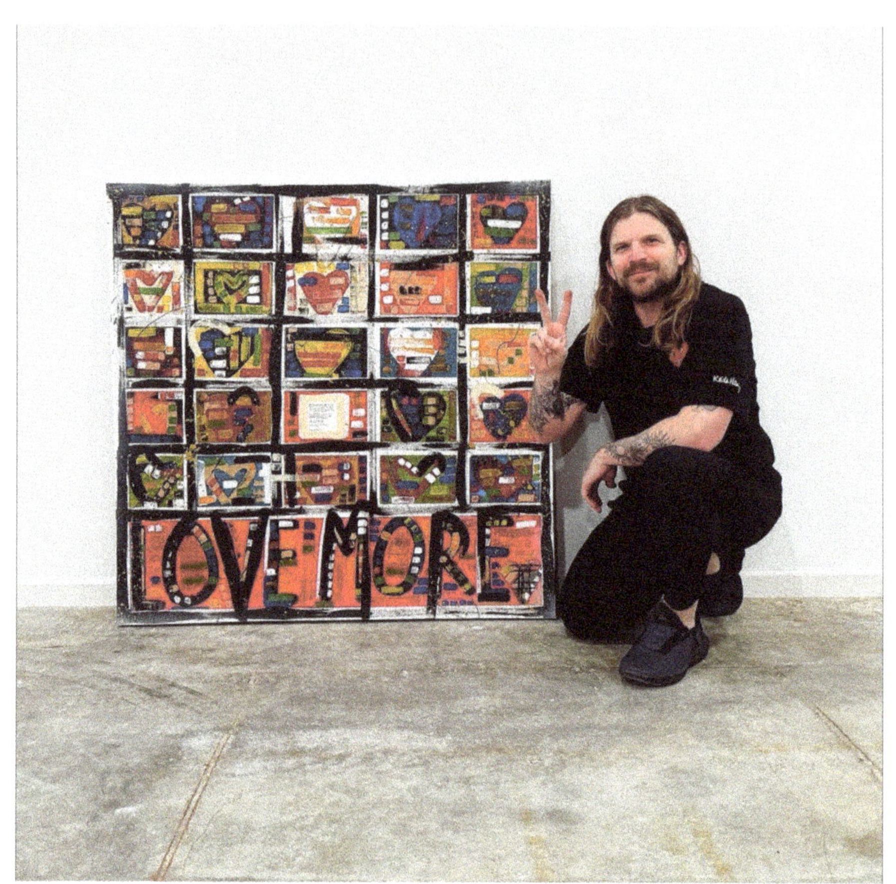

LOVE MORE

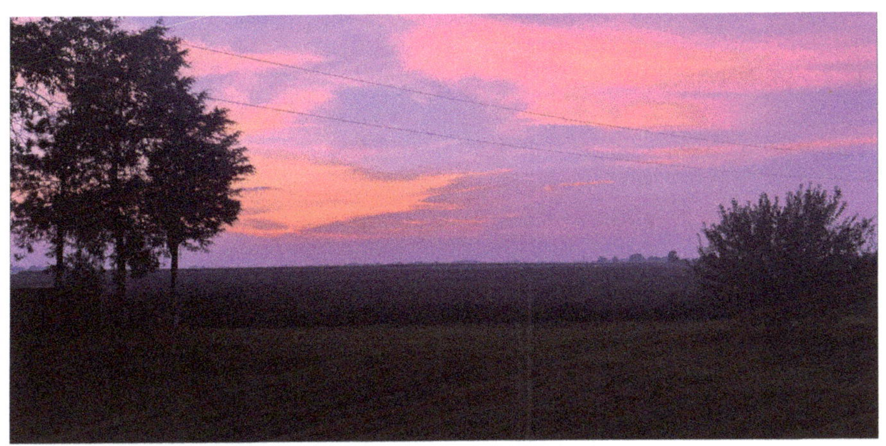

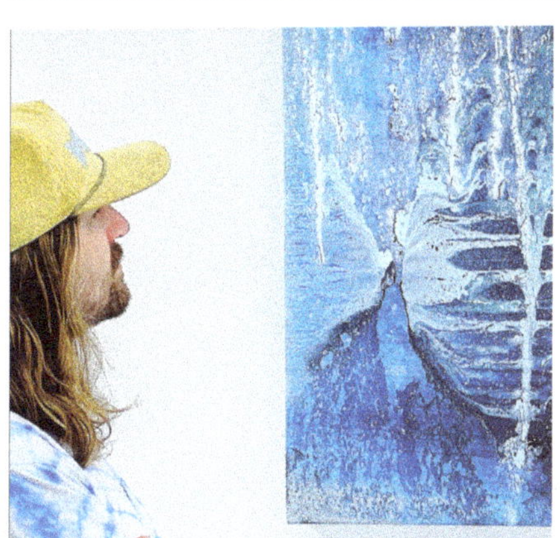

the coffee hits
my lips, i breathe
in the fresh morning
air, and i am reminded
how beautiful it is
to simply be alive.

/ topher kearby

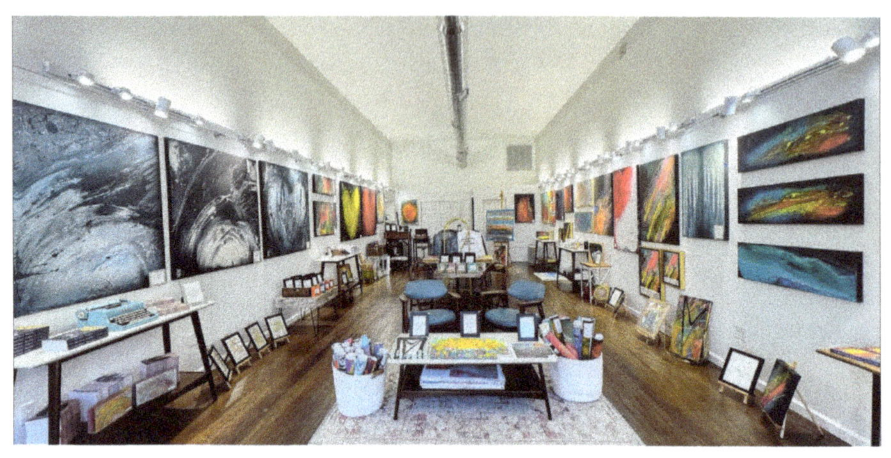

WHEN WE DREAM WITH OUR FULL POWER
WE WAKE THE UNIVERSE AND LET OUR FUTURE
KNOW WE ARE ON OUR WAY.

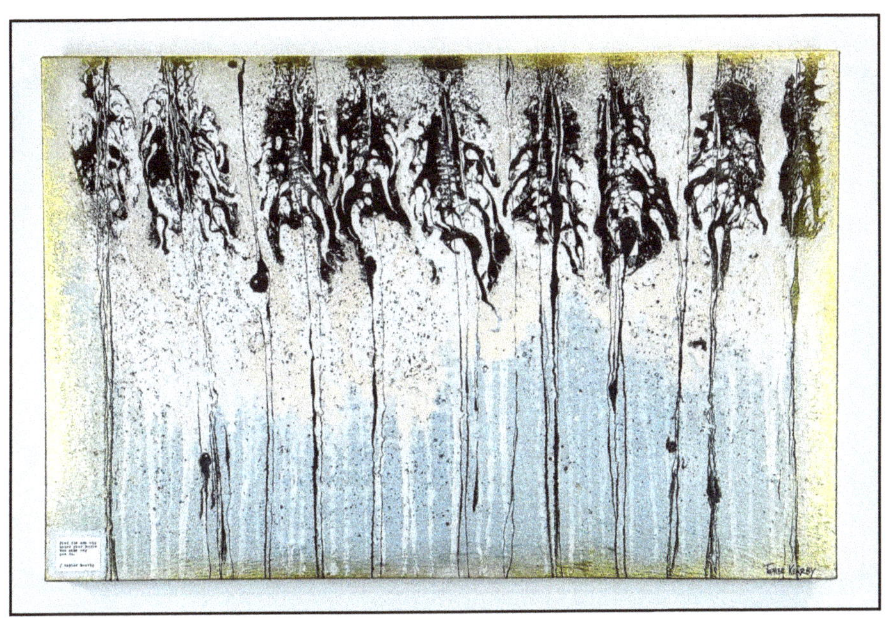

you can love who you
are — today. and still
be excited by the wild
and wonderful person
you are becoming.

life is not stagnant.
it is fluid and ever
changing —

and so are we.

/ topher kearby

you aren't starting over. you're
starting from where you are at.
with all that you have learned.
with every experience. all the
tools you have gathered during
your life. for this moment.
for right now.

so don't be discouraged if you
feel like you are taking a step
back. this time is important. it
is so you can clear your mind,
steady your heart, and prepare
yourself for the next part of
your journey.

/ topher kearby

the morning settles in and once
again i am carried away by the
spirit of a new day. hope fills
my heart and wonder ignites my
imagination with all of the
possibilities of what could be.

i am thankful for this life and
the days i get to live. and i am
excited for the experiences that
i am moving towards.

the coffee is hot.
the music is playing.
and everything feels
just as it's meant to be.

a new day is here.
and i am ready.

/ topher kearby

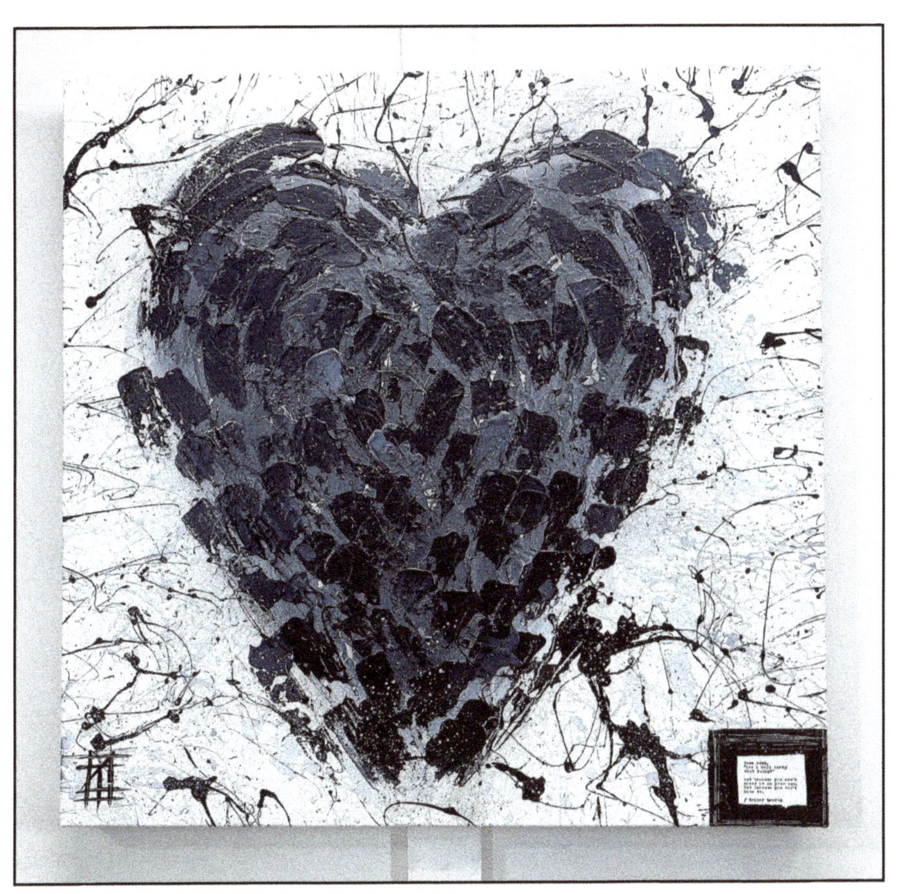

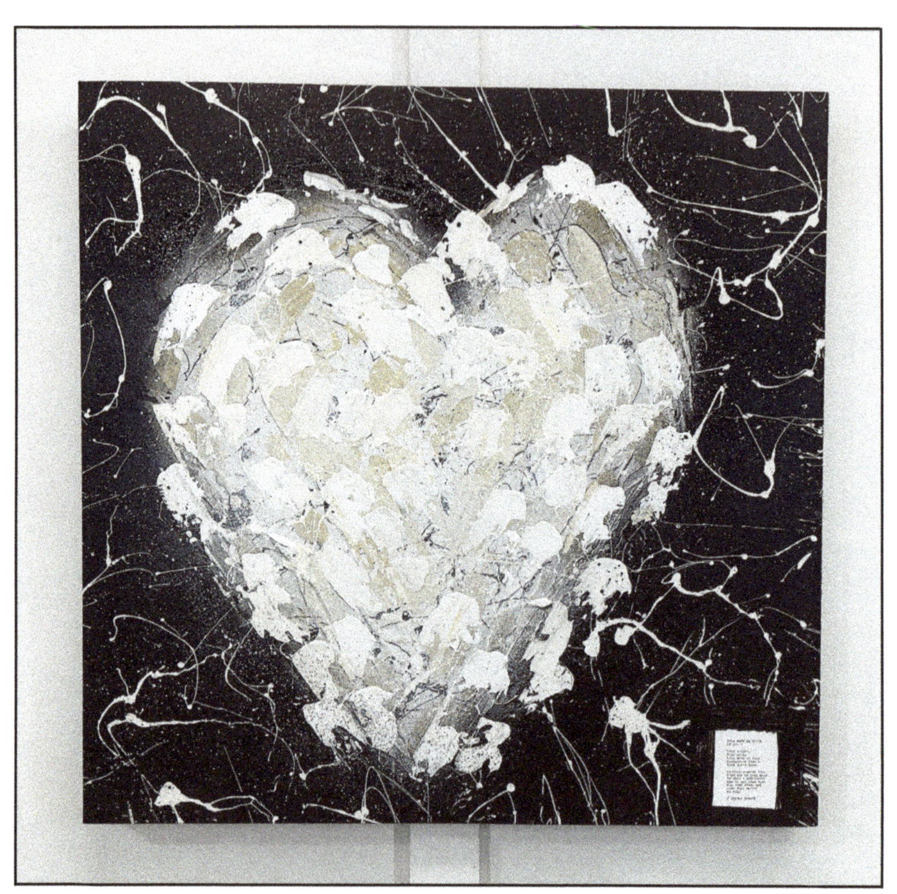

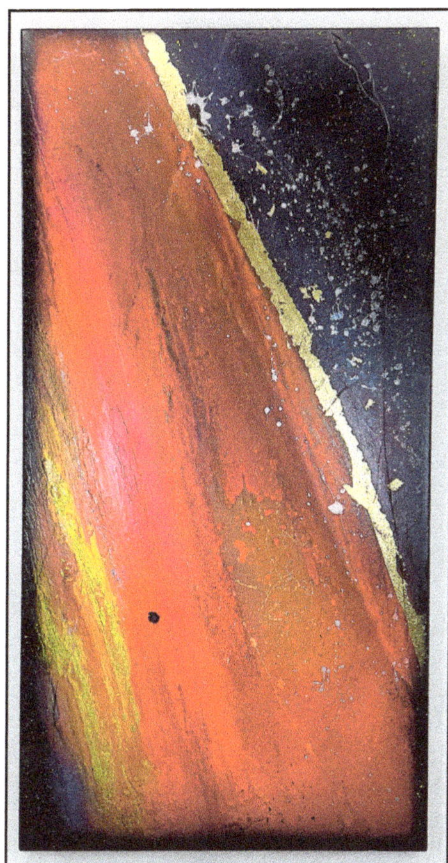

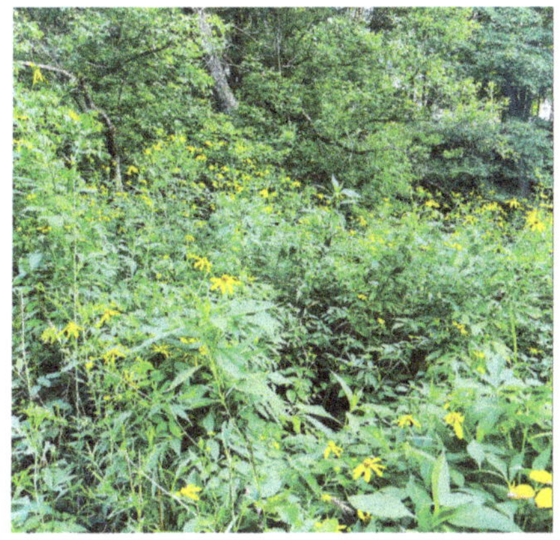

helping people to feel a lot
more loved and understood in
this life is a really good use
of our time.

/ topher kearby

HOPE IS A GIFT WE CAN SHARE WITH OTHERS
THAT DOESN'T COST A DIME AND CAN MAKE AN IMPACT
THAT LASTS FAR BEYOND OUR LIFETIME.

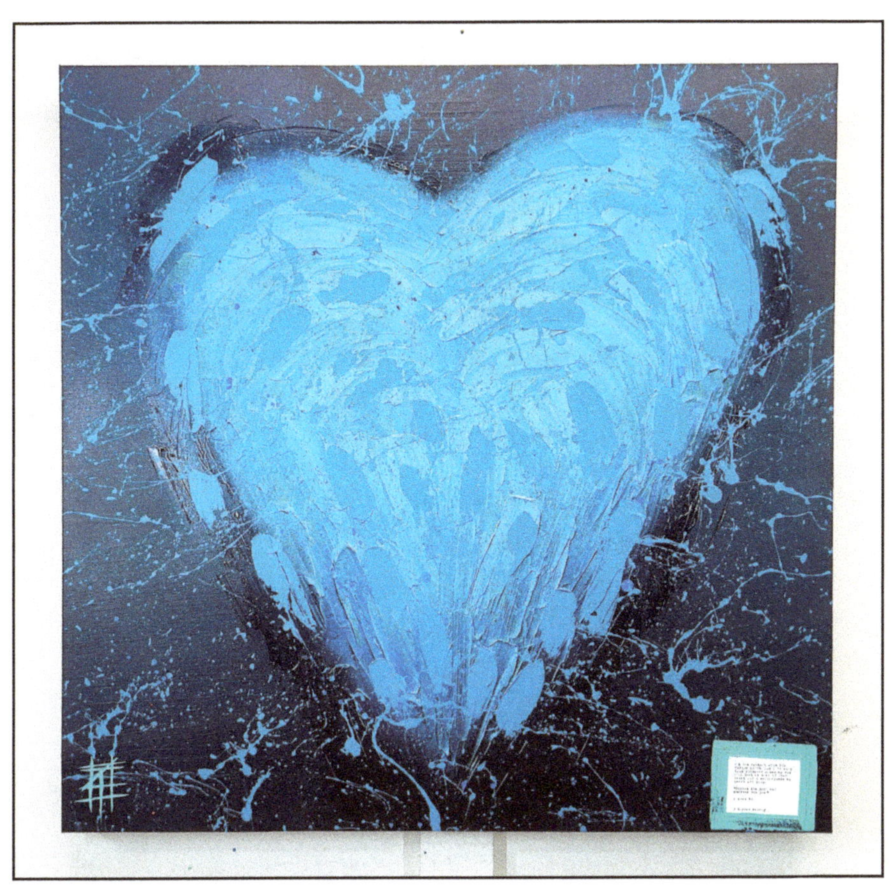

HOPEFUL TRAVELER

i'm not certain what the
future holds. but i do know
that whatever comes my way
i'll meet it with an open
heart and a willingness to
learn and grow.

"follow the good and
embrace the joy."

i plan to.

/ topher kearby

the journey to where
we need to be in life
often travels through
our insecurities.

not to make us question
who we are – but to remind
us who we can be.

/ topher kearby

a new day does not
begin with the sunrise;
it begins with a new way
of thinking — fresh eyes.

/ topher kearby

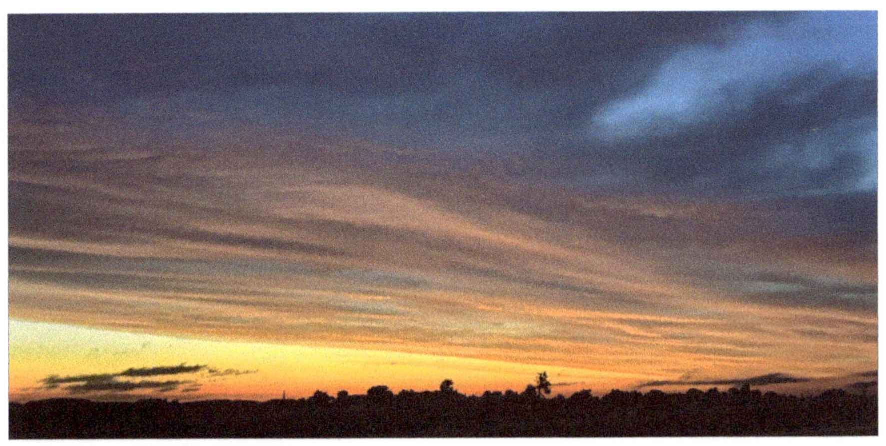

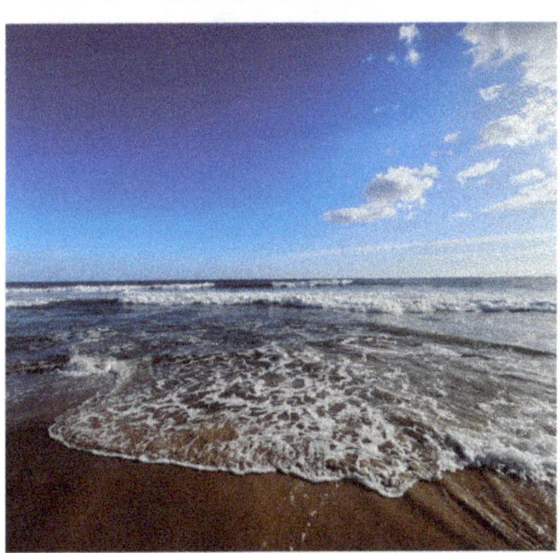

wake and dream.
plan and hope.
fill your mind
with wonder.
fill your heart
with passion.

make today the
best day of
your life.

/ topher kearby

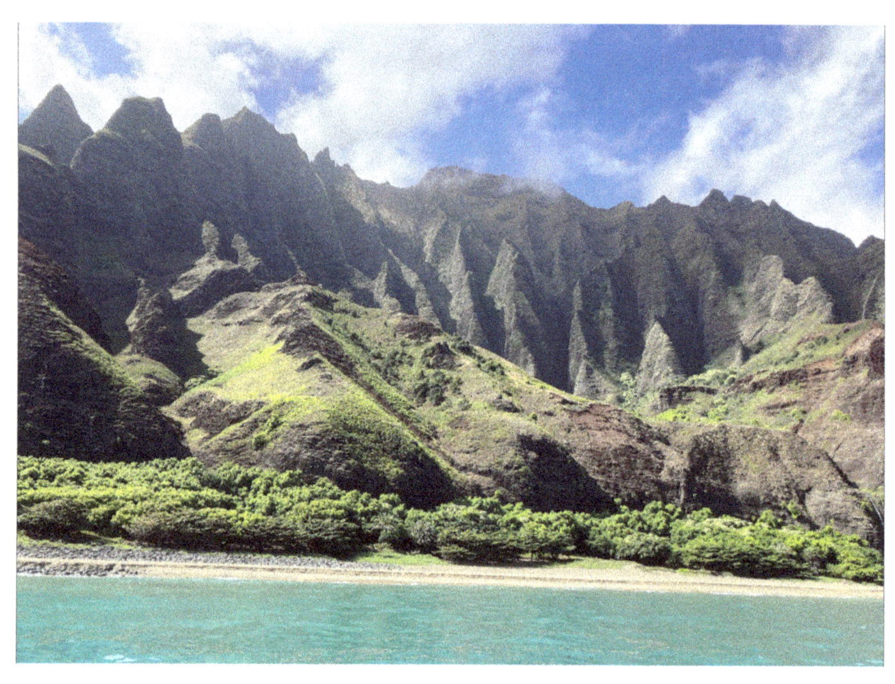

WE OFTEN DREAM OF BETTER DAYS IN THE FUTURE
AT THE EXPENSE OF OUR PRESENT MOMENTS –
IT'S MORE FULFILLING TO LIVE IN THE PRESENT.

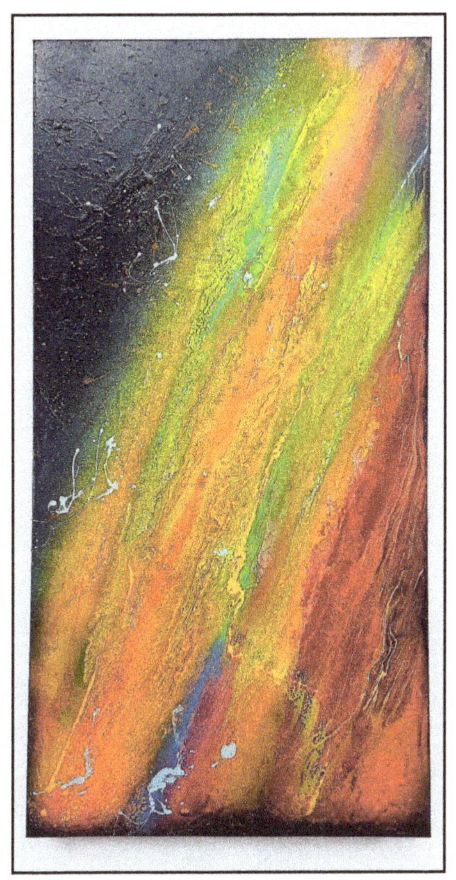

HOPEFUL TRAVELER

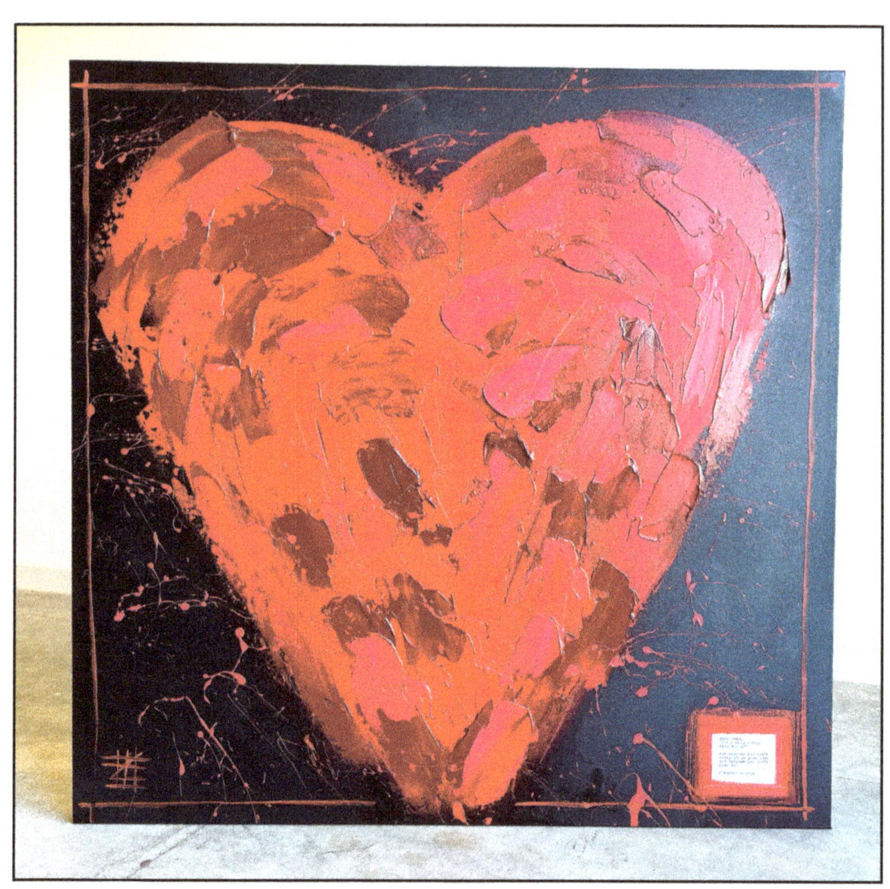

choosing situations that are
good for you takes courage.
situations that are loving,
healing, and encourage you
to feel hopeful.

because those places are
often off the normal paths
in life. and sometimes you
must travel them alone.

but the journey is worth
every difficult moment
and every unsure step.

because the rewards is
a life well lived.

/ topher kearby

when you live with kindness
you become connected to life
in such a meaningful way.
because you are no longer
approaching situations from
just an inward point of view.
instead you are seeing the
world as it is - a place that
needs love and support. and
people for who they are -
individuals who long to be
seen and understood.

that kind of perspective
changes everything.

/ topher kearby

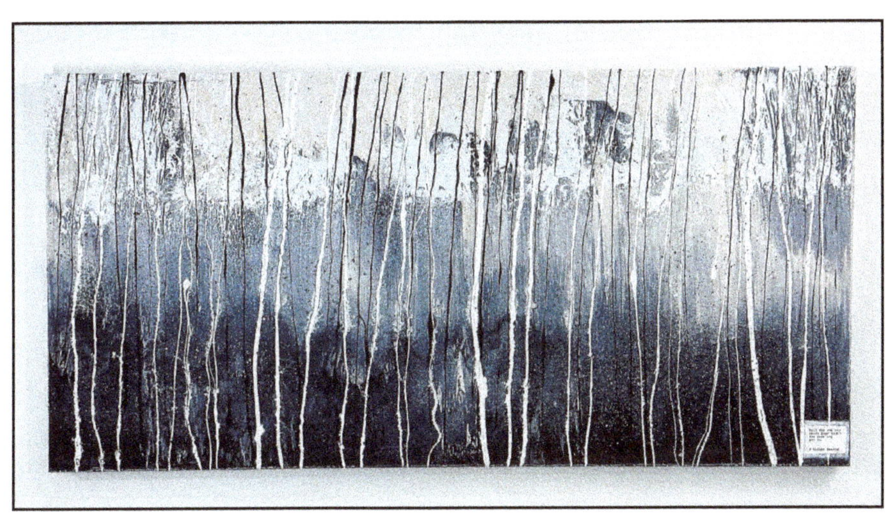

HOPEFUL TRAVELER

most people want
something from you.

the best people bring
something out of you.

and that's a very
different thing.

/ topher kearby

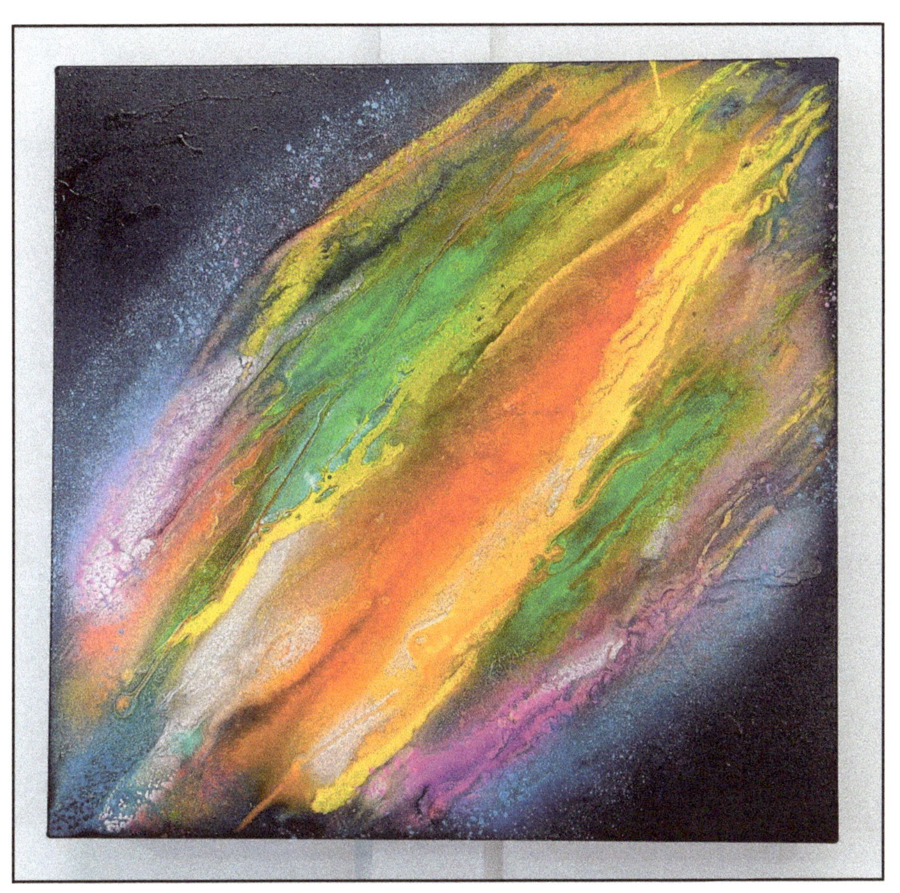

HOPEFUL TRAVELER

when we love people as
they are, where they are,
for who they are - life
becomes simple. no longer
are assumptions clouding
our vision. because we see
that people are doing the
best with what they have
been given.

forgiveness replaces
resentment. and kindness
overcomes any judgments.

it's a better way to live
and it keeps life simple -
love first, love more, and
appreciate people for who
they really are.

/ topher kearby

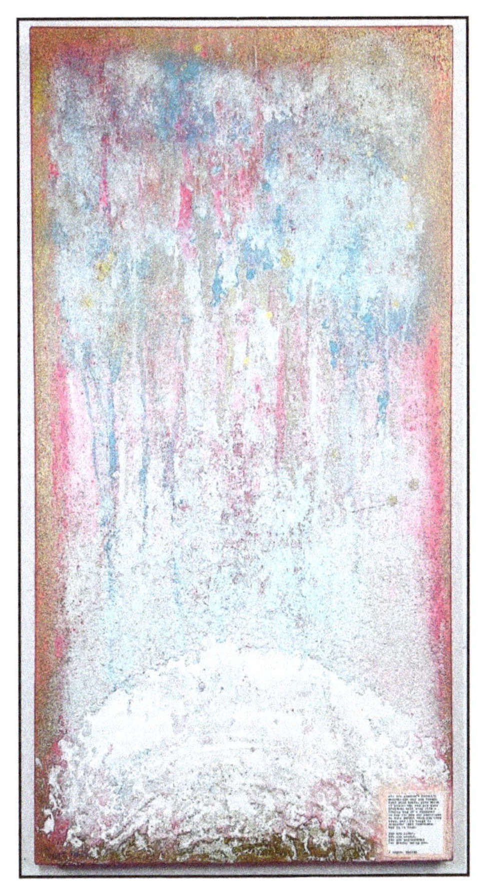

i'm looking ahead.
i'm making no excuses.
i see the future that
i want and i'm willing
to work for it.
whatever it takes.
setbacks won't stop me.
negative voices won't
break my spirit.
my mind is set.
my heart is willing.
nothing is going to
stand in my way.

my time is now.

/ topher kearby

"authenticity is
freedom."

choices become clearer,
interactions with other
people become more soulful,
and life becomes more
meaningful.

not because there
are no challenges,
but because you know
that what you need to
meet each new situation
is within you.

/ topher kearby

life gives us
opportunities to
let go of who we
are not so that we
may know who we
are more clearly.

/ topher kearby

your tenderness is a
gift, your gentle heart
is a strength, and your
willingness to see the
best in people is a
light that this world
desperately needs.

don't dull your fire
just because it makes
others uncomfortable.

/ topher kearby

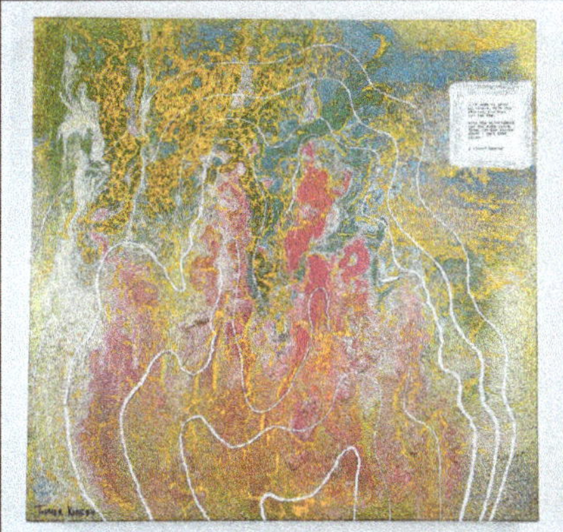

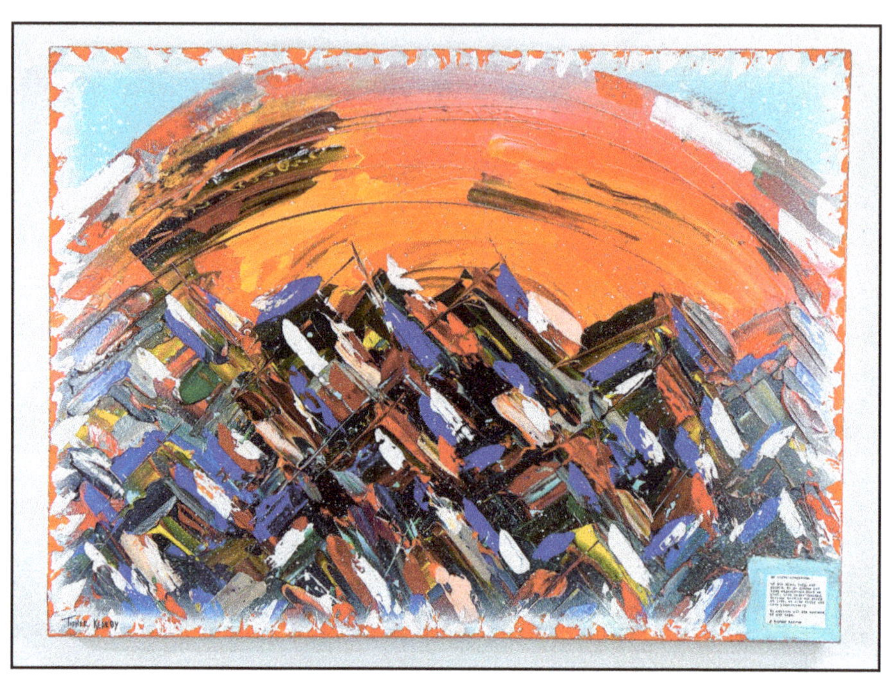

BE AN ADVENTURE SEEKER. A WILD WORLD TRAVELER.
SOMEONE WHO BELIEVES THAT MAKING THE IMPOSSIBLE
HAPPEN IS JUST A NORMAL PART OF LIFE.

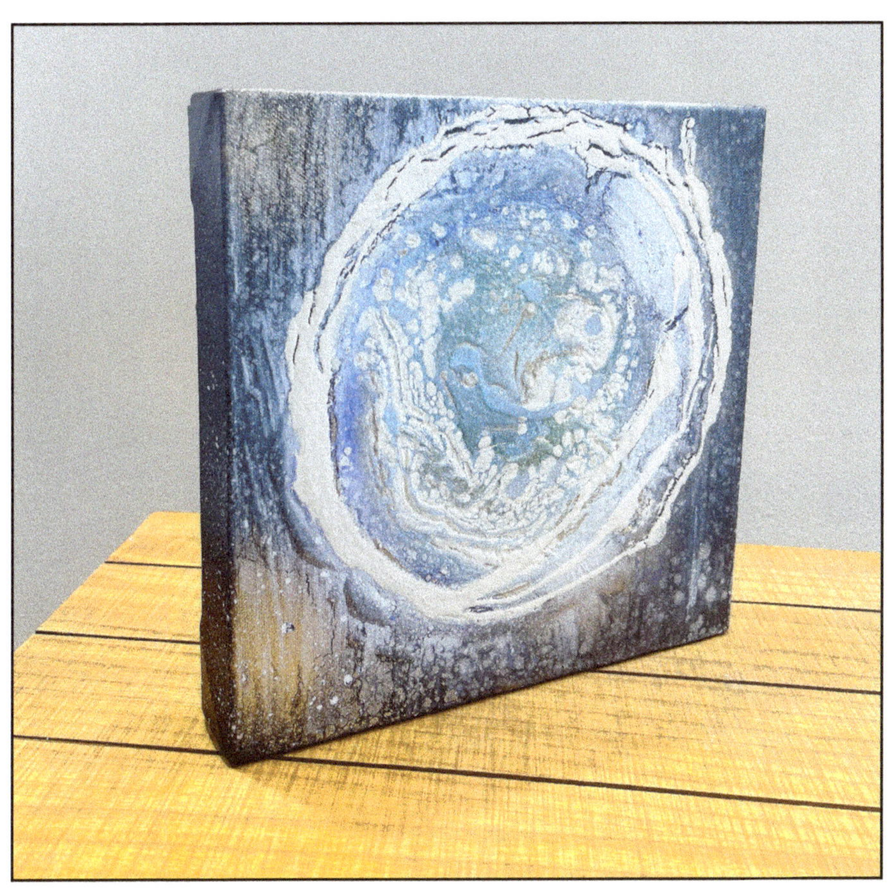

i bought her
flowers not
because she
needed them,
but because
i needed her.

/ topher kearby

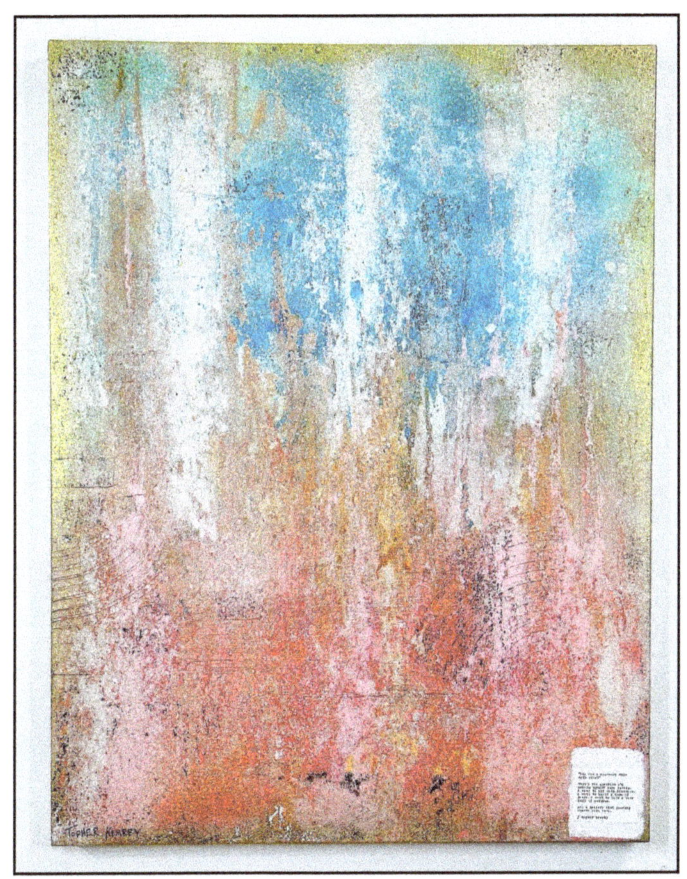

sometimes healing looks
a lot like sitting still,
lying down, not speaking,
not moving, and not being
able to process anything
other than the weight of
the universe pressing into
your chest.

don't rush that time;
those feelings are
important.

/ topher kearby

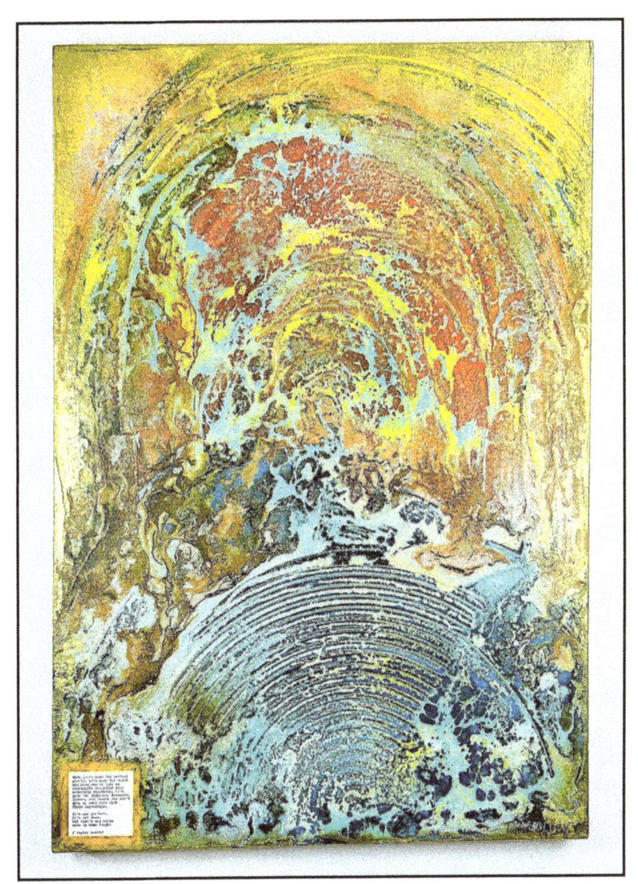

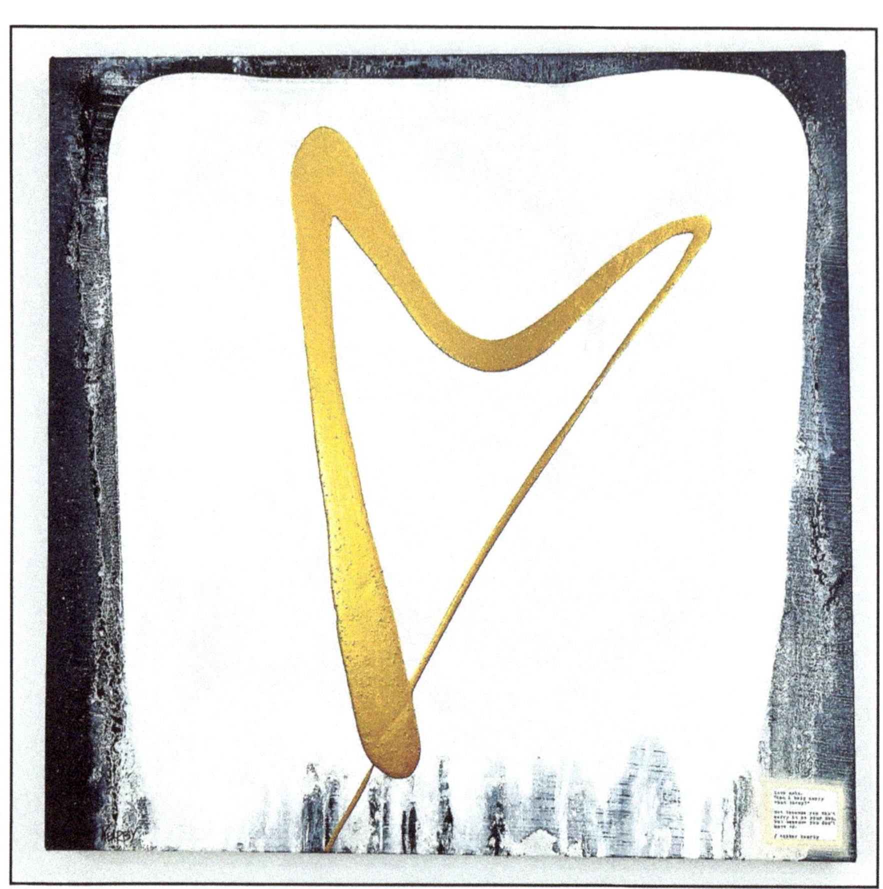

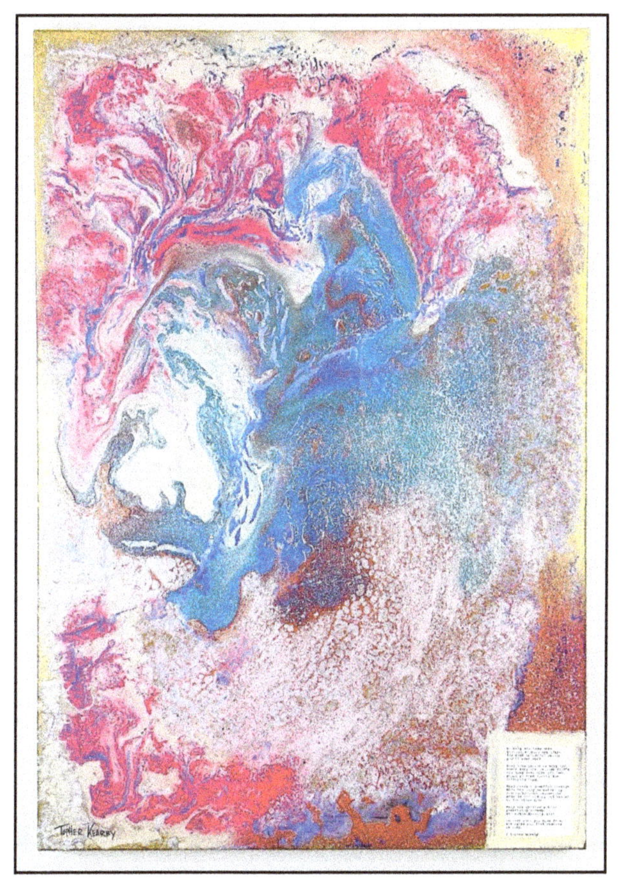

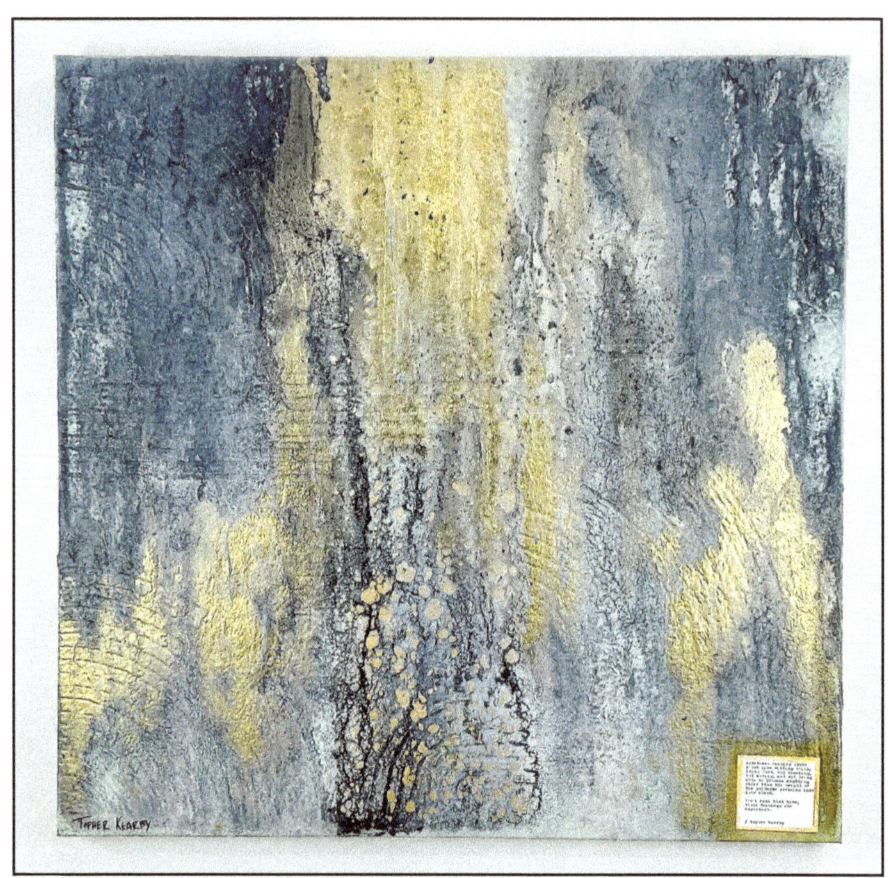

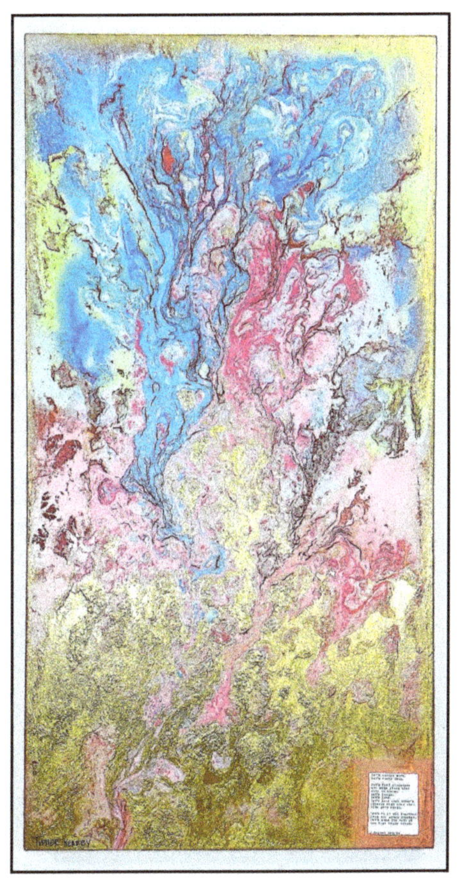

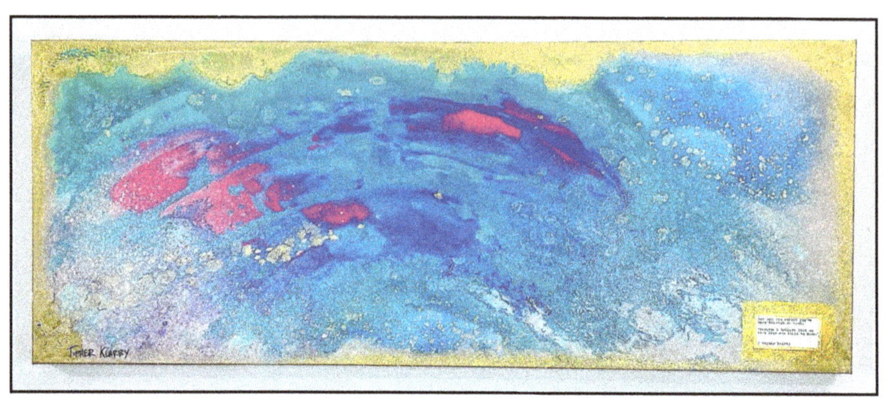

THE WINDS AND THE WAVES,
THE SKY AND THE SEAS,
WHEN I AM ONE WITH NATURE
IS WHEN I AM FINALLY FREE.

you are a bright and beautiful
light. you shine for everyone
in your life and each person
you meet is better for it -
because of your kindness
and your love.

generosity is your language
and you speak it every day.

there may be easier paths to
take, but for you - there is
no better way.

/ topher kearby

i am thankful for
this wild heart and
this creative mind.
for they allow me to
see past the limitations
of this moment. and look
ahead to a future filled
with endless potential
and infinite possibilities.

/ topher kearby

we crave adventure.

of the mind, body, and
spirit. to go places and
have experiences that we
could have never dreamed.
because that is the story
of life. to live fully and
love passionately.

to embrace all the wonders
of our days.

/ topher kearby

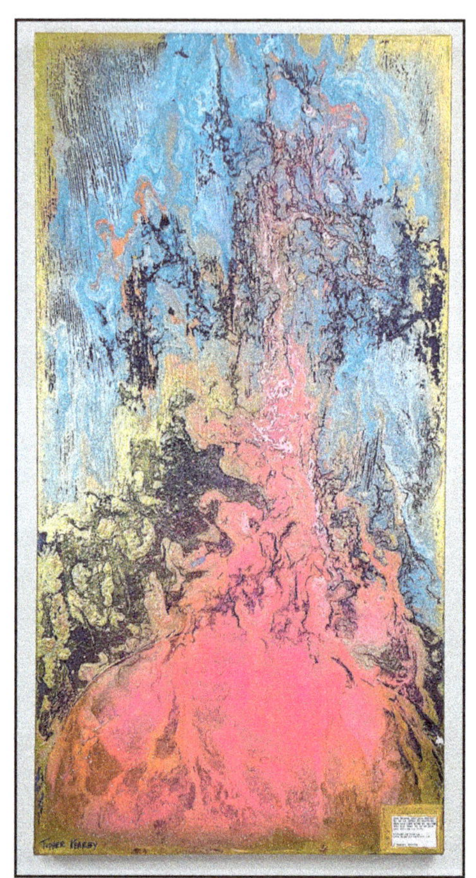

Tipper Pearcy

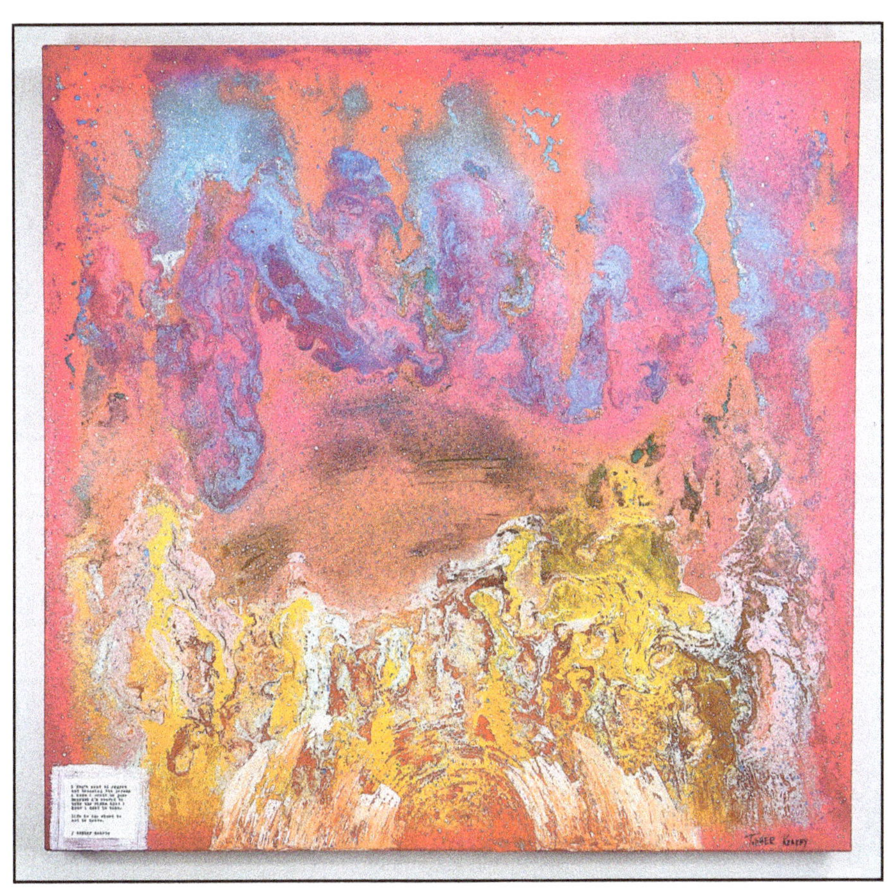

i don't want to regret
not becoming the person
i know i could be just
because i'm scared to
take the risks that i
know i need to take.

life is too short to
not be brave.

/ topher kearby

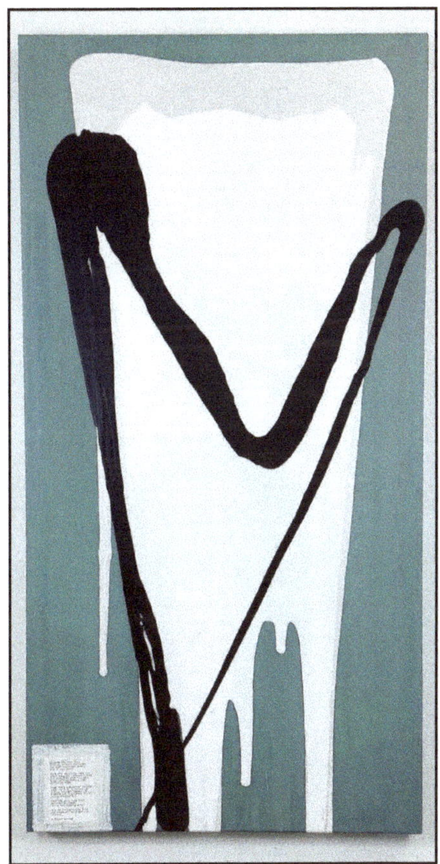

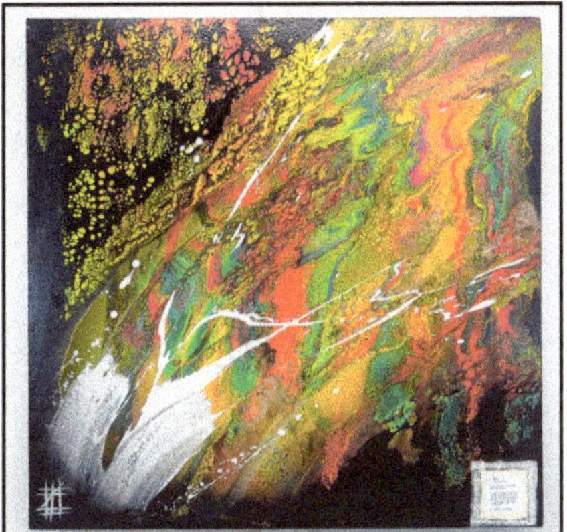

if you spend your time
waiting for the perfect
moment when everything
will feel right, you'll
end up wasting all of
the imperfect moments
that make up this
beautiful life.

/ topher kearby

TRUE STRENGTH iS SETTING BOUNDARiES
THAT HELP YOU TO GROW IN WAYS THAT ARE TRUE
TO YOURSELF AND YOUR PURPOSE.

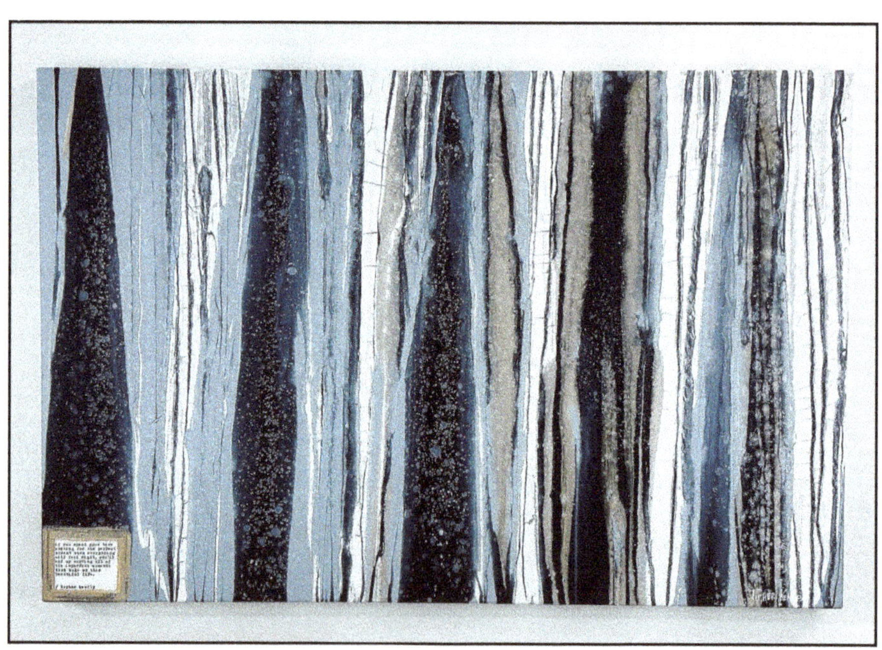

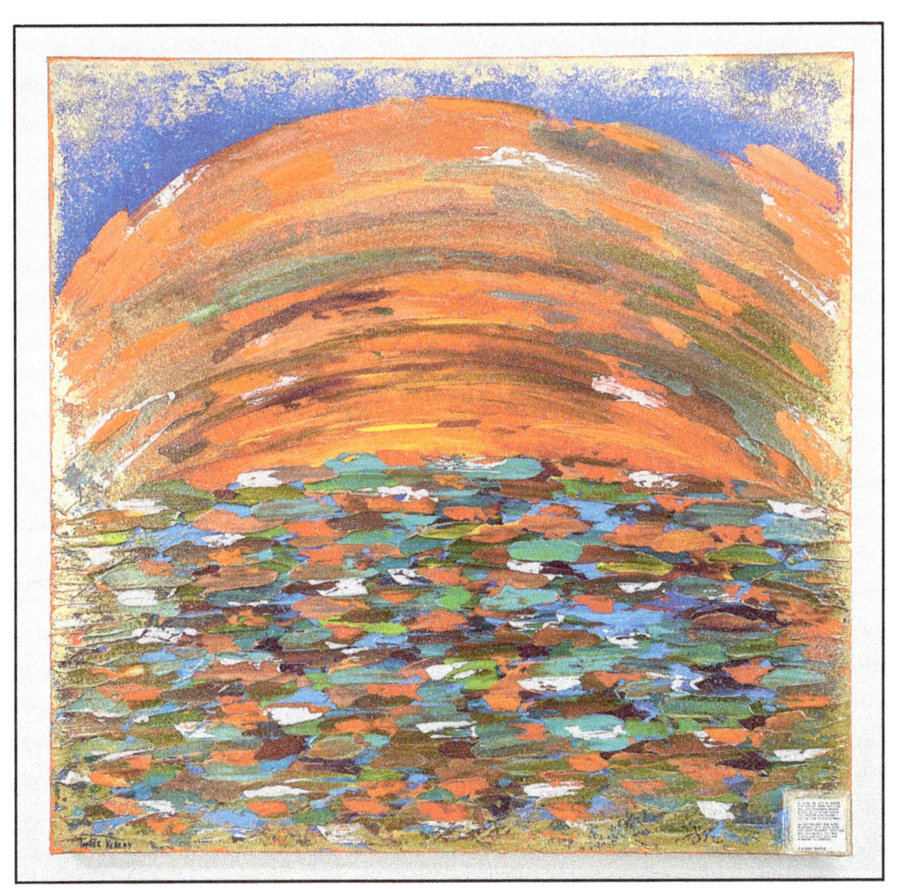

HOPEFUL **TRAVELER**

go with me now to where
our dreams meet reality
and our forevers start
today. to a place where
our hearts are happy -
and we are finally seen.

we can travel the path
together. for this life
and into forever. through
the beautiful and the
difficult and all the
moments in between.

/ topher kearby

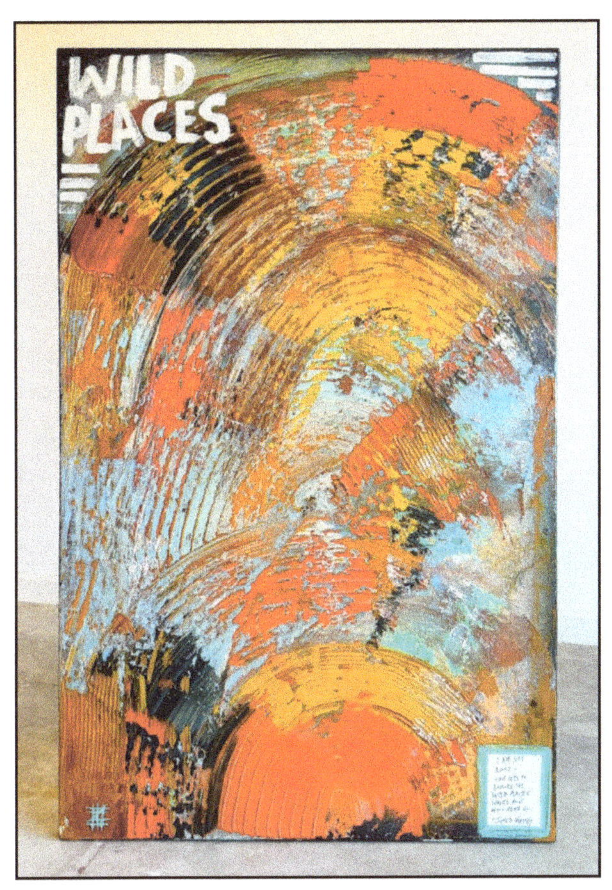

WILD
PLACES

when the flowers start
to bloom and the winds
begin to move.

when i am in tune with
nature - the world around
me feels brand new.

/ topher kearby

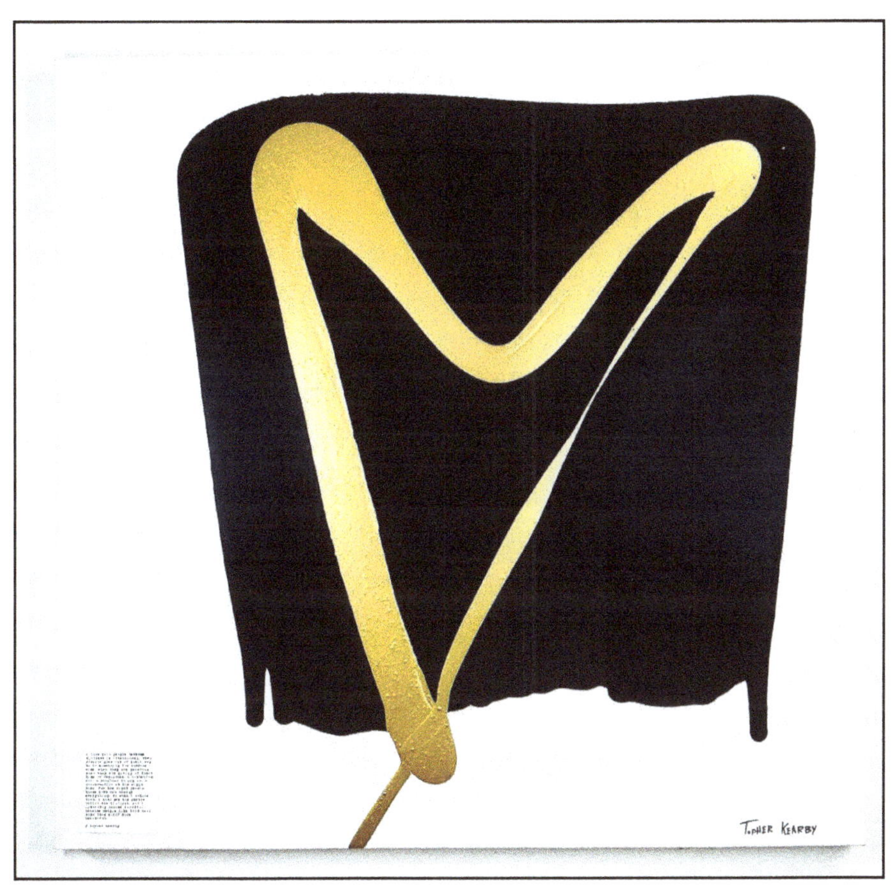

Topher Kearby

Love is so often associated with romantic relationships. And of course it is. Songs, poems, art, and media are all about the impact that romantic love makes in our lives - because it is so important.

But most of the connections we have in life are different.

Love is also friendships, family, and our interactions with complete strangers.

We all want to be seen and appreciated for who we are – no matter what the situation is.

"How would this interaction go if I loved this person?"

That's a thought I recycle in my mind. Maybe I am waiting in line, stuck in traffic, or just being presented with a difficult situation. My instinct might be to be unkind to whoever is the "cause" of the delay.

But when I choose to do my best and lead with love it completely changes my energy.

Every difficult situations changes from one of frustration to one where I can be loving.

Yes, it is good for others, but it also helps me heal.

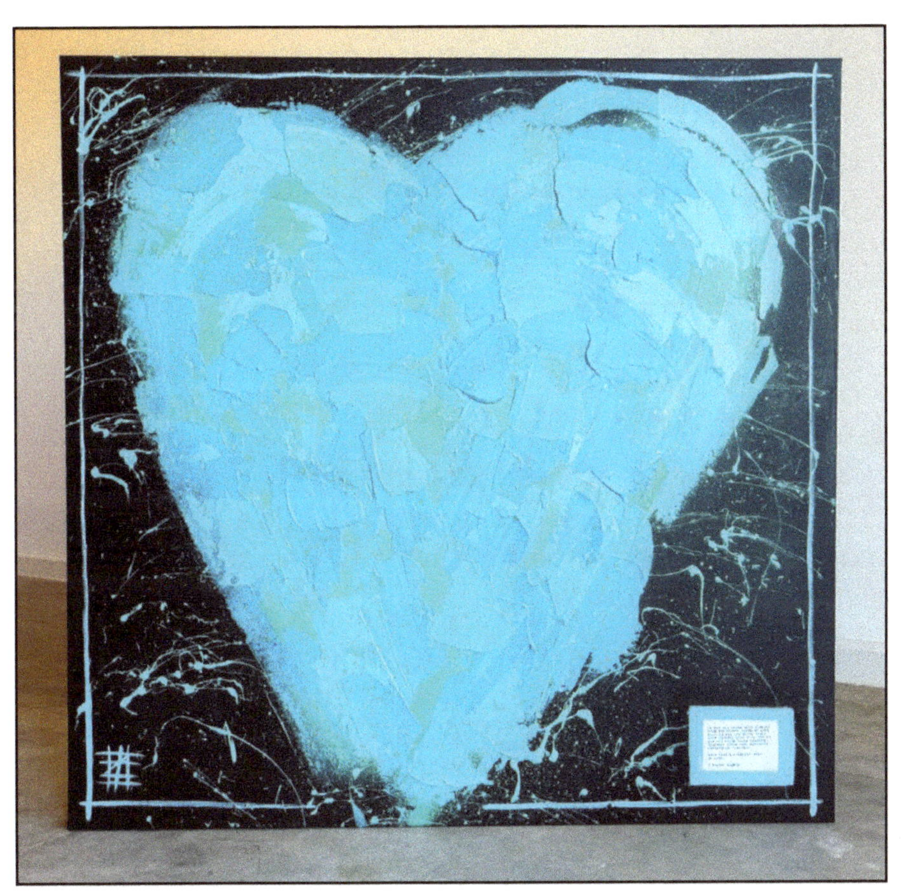

HOPEFUL TRAVELER

i used to see the difficult
days that i have lived as
wasted — i was just doing
what i needed to do to make
it through.

i survived.

but now i see them more
as time well spent — i was
growing into the person i
am today.

now i am ready to thrive.

/ topher kearby

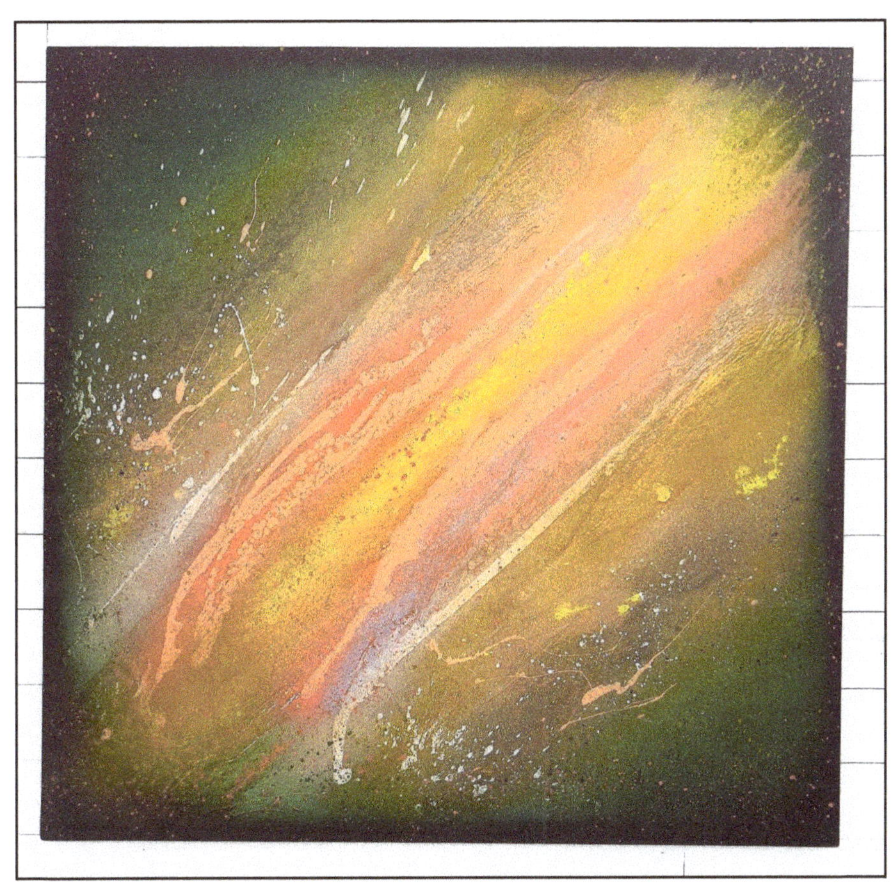

HOPEFUL **TRAVELER**

deep soulful conversations
can heal so many unseen
wounds and calm so many
restless worries.

/ topher kearby

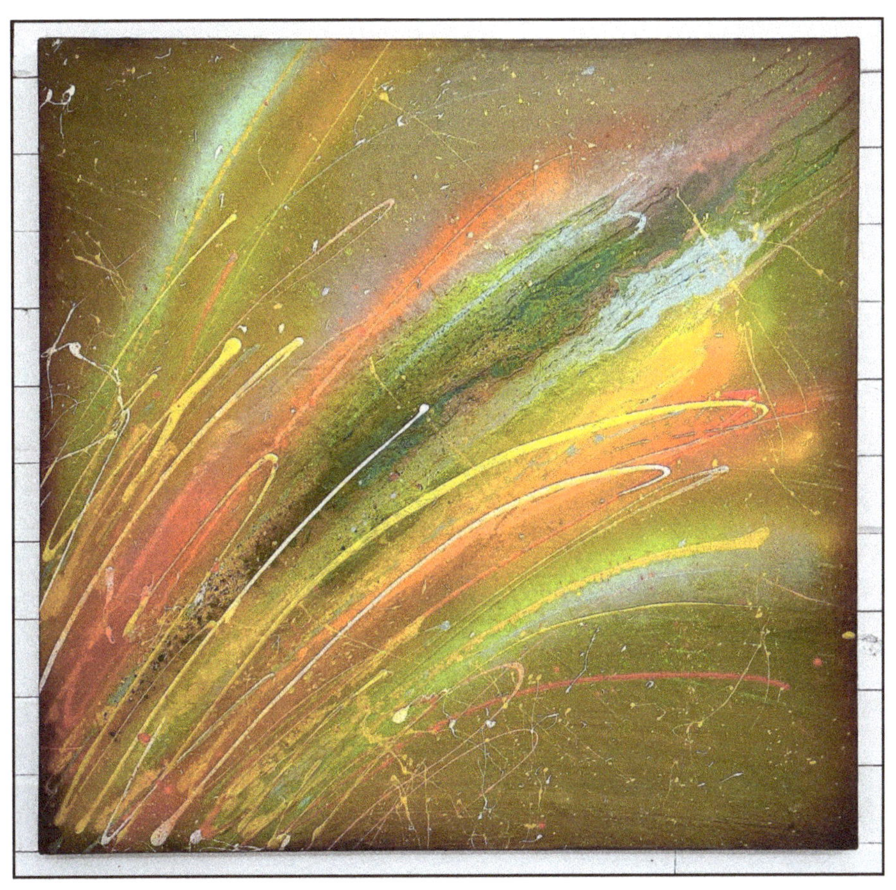

HOPEFUL **TRAVELER**

you are stronger
than you think,
more powerful
than you know,
and this world
is lucky to have
your unique energy.

/ topher kearby

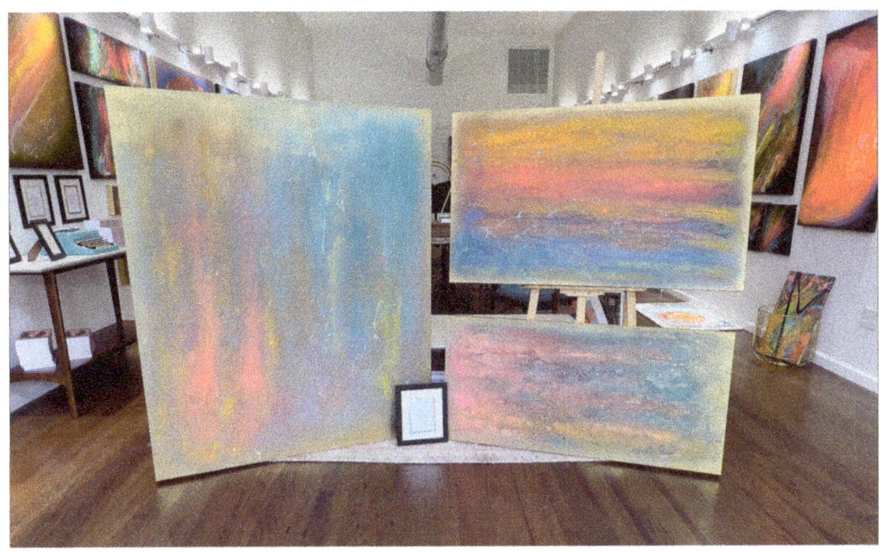

There are so many lessons we can learn from trees. Learning more about how they grow and live has been a life long passion of mine. That's because I see such beauty in their ability to grow exactly where they are with the resources that surround them.

Personally, that is a lesson that has taken me so many years to appreciate and understand.

I was constantly moving and searching for a place or space to find my happiness. I needed so many other things other than what was surrounding me in order to feel content. At least, that is what I believed. Some of that is simply how humans are wired – we are wandering creatures and that is beautiful. Yet, there is so much peace in learning to growth with your surroundings.

To look around you and say, "All I need is all around me."

That's an incredible affirmation.

Trees also know how to work together. The survival of the fittest idea isn't always true with forests, They share with one another, communicate, and protect younger saplings from growing too fast. Yes, they are all in a race toward the light but they also understand how each part of the community is needed.

What a beautiful world we can create if we all lived the same way – to reflect, recharge, and express gratitude for everything that had happened during the day.

healing takes time —
and it also takes a
lot of love.

love from others —
that may look like
understanding, help,
forgiveness, or simply
being there.

love from yourself —
that may look like
personal time, rest,
spiritual and physical
development, or going
on a new adventure.

the journey is unique
for everyone but we all
need time and love to
make it through.

/ topher kearby

through witnessing the
beauty of the "every day"
moments that are so easy
to miss —

we understand that life
is so much more than just
the "big events."

it's the moments
"in between"
that truly give life a
fullness and add so much
purpose to our days.

/ topher kearby

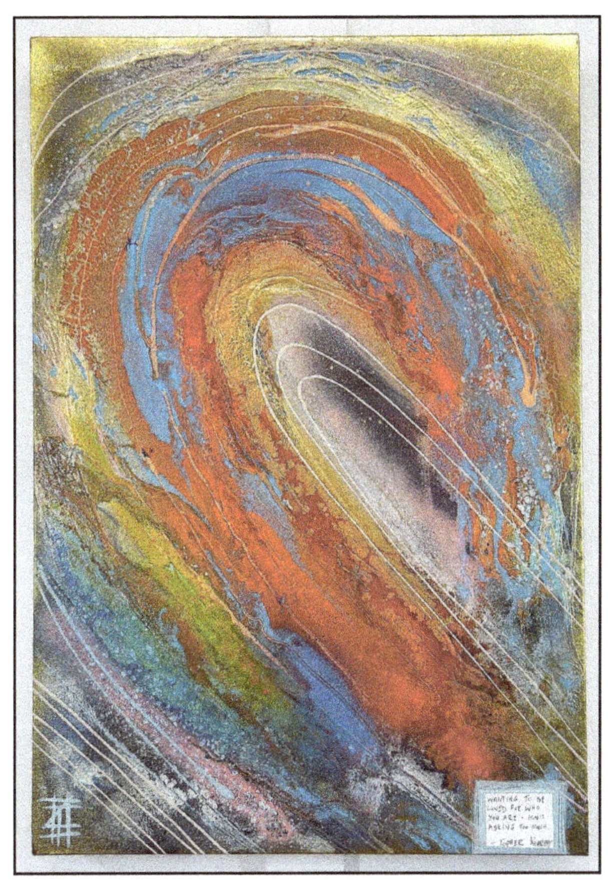
WANTING TO BE
LOVED FOR WHO
YOU ARE - ISN'T
ASKING TOO MUCH.
- GARTH NIXON

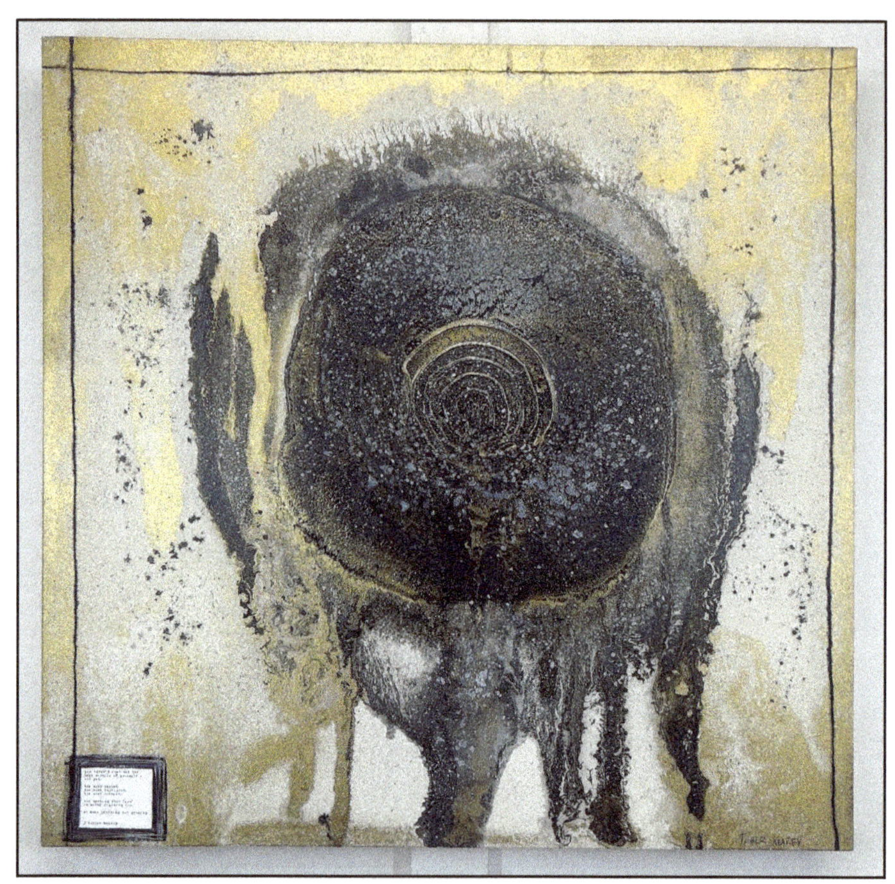

let's wander more.
let's worry less.

let's find adventure,
and make plans that
make no sense.

let's laugh.
let's love.
let's keep each other's
spirits high even when
life gets rough.

let's do it all
together.
from now until
forever,
let's make the rest of
our days truly count.

/ topher kearby

There is power in nature.

Simply taking a walk in the woods can alter our state of mind in such a positive way. The forest has a way of teaching us by simply "being."

The trees are no more and no less than they are required to be. They stand alone but work together in community in order to thrive.

That's a lesson we can all take to heart. We are individuals but we are also part of something more. The way we interact with one another matters. It can be a simple kindness made in passing, or a major effort to help make real change in someone's life. The resources we have and talents we are given can be used to do so much good in the world once we realize we are here to experience this life together.

Never underestimate the impact your life can make for others.

I think about how the plumb tree in my backyard has been home to a small family of birds this summer. The tree was growing on its own. It needed, sun, water, and nutrients to become what it was meant to be. But still it was able to help others along their journey while it grew –

I love that.

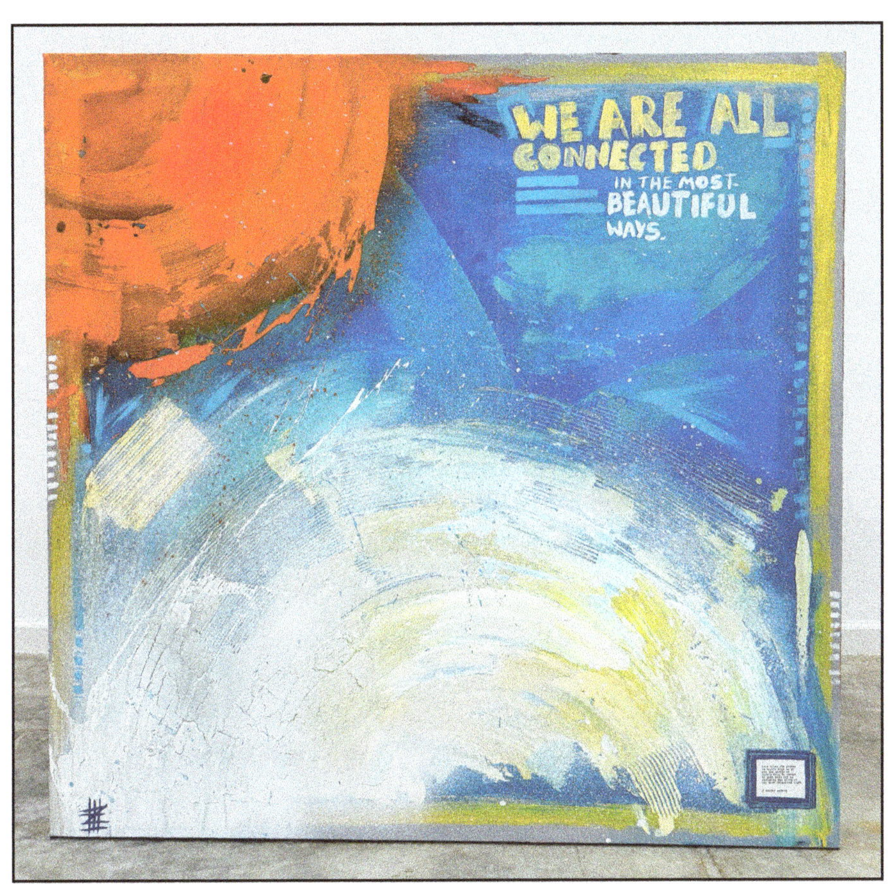

WE ARE ALL
CONNECTED
IN THE MOST
BEAUTIFUL
WAYS.

it's often the places
we didn't plan to go
and the people we
didn't know we needed
to meet that end up
changing our lives in
the most beautiful ways.

/ topher kearby

we pursue so many things
to make us happy. but all
we really need is time.

time to reflect and learn.
time to talk and understand.
time away from distractions.
and time doing what we love
with the people we love.

life doesn't always make it
easy to prioritize these
choices. but it's worth the
effort to reclaim our time.

/ topher kearby

the journey is unique
for everyone, but we all
need time and love to
make through.

/ topher kearby

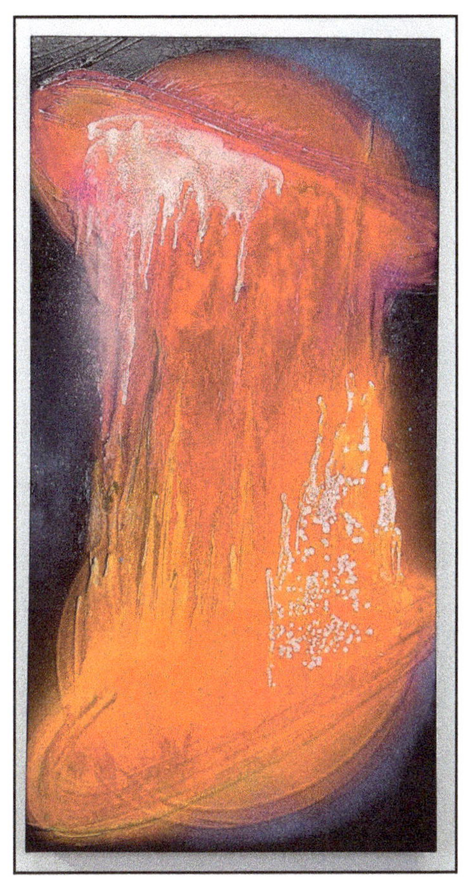

HOPEFUL **TRAVELER**

when you spend your life feeling
misunderstood. out of place. as if
the frequency you send off isn't
picked up by anyone. the song of
your heart isn't heard by others
in the same way you hear it.

it can be lonely.

but then there comes a day when
someone picks up on your energy.
they hear your music. and for the
first time in your life you feel
heard. understood. seen. and that
connection is more powerful than
almost anything.

so if you find it or if you have
it - hold it close. because that's
a rare type of magic that should
never be wasted.

/ topher kearby

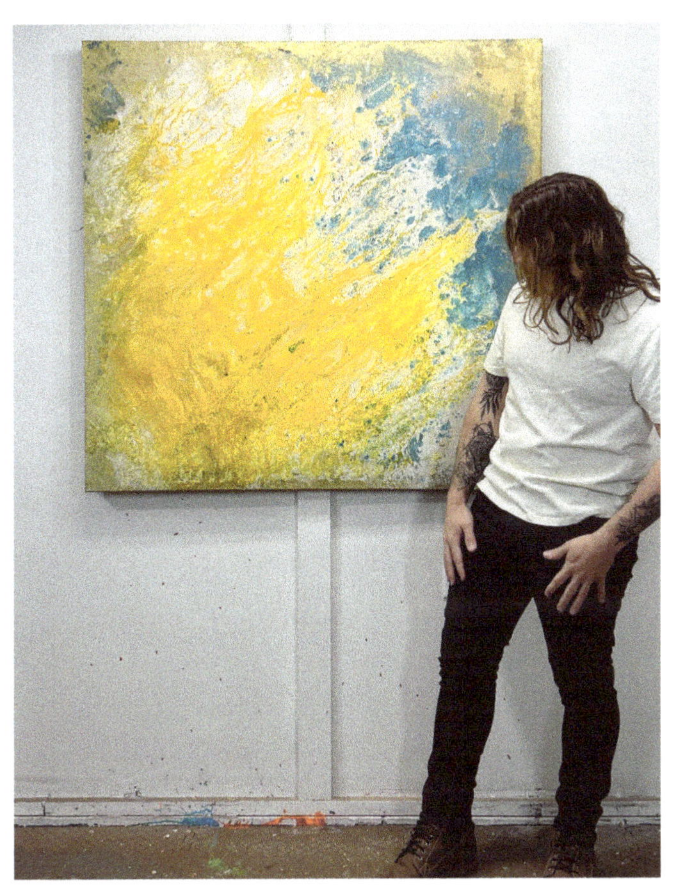

"Life can be difficult, painful, and downright impossible at times.

But it is also so beautiful, important – and worth it."

It has been a few years since my last book and I'm happy to share these pages with all of you. The stories we share with one another matter and the more open we can be with our journeys helps everyone feel more seen and understood.

Find art, books, prints, or schedule a gallery visit at www.topherkearby.com.

Please send all questions or business inquiries to topherkearby@gmail.com.

BE A HOPEFUL TRAVELER –
SOMEONE WHO UNDERSTANDS THAT
LIFE IS MORE ABOUT THE JOURNEY
THAN THE DESTINATION.

www.ingramcontent.com/pod-product-compliance
Lightning Source LLC
Chambersburg PA
CBHW041830110726
48006CB00020B/2573